DO YOU KNOW THE

FUTURE?

GOD`S PLAN FROM PRESENT TO ETERNAL STATE

DO YOU KNOW THE FUTURE?

GOD'S PLAN FROM PRESENT TO ETERNAL STATE

JOE S. PHILIP

DO YOU KNOW YOUR FUTURE:
GOD'S PLAN FROM PRESENT TO ETERNAL STATE
By: Joel S. Philip
Copyright © 2014
GOSPEL FOLIO PRESS
All Rights Reserved

Published by
GOSPEL FOLIO PRESS
304 Killaly St. W.
Port Colborne, ON L3K 6A6
CANADA

ISBN: 9781927521588

Cover design by Danielle Elzinga

All Scripture quotations from the
King James Version unless otherwise noted.

Printed in CANADA

ACKNOWLEDGMENTS

Beth Paul for her editorial services and suggestions.
With special thanks to my dear wife, Nisha, who has encouraged me in the Lord's work and to my loving parents (Papa and Mummy), Philip & Ponnamma.

CONTENTS

Introduction 9

ONE   The Reliability of the Bible 11

TWO   The Rapture 23

THREE   The Tribulation Period 39

FOUR   The Millenial Kingdom 93

FIVE   The Eternal State 129

SIX   How Do You Fit into God's Plan? 139

Appendix 145

INTRODUCTION

Some might think, how could a book that was written over 3400 years ago contain the future events that are going to take place in the world? It talks about such things because it is the inspired Word of God. It is the lack of knowledge of what the future holds and our inability to accurately predict the future that jeopardizes our life. In our daily lives we struggle to make important decisions because we don't know what tomorrow holds. That is why the Bible is so vital to our lives. Not only does the Bible contain historical accounts of events, but it gives a panoramic view of God's future plan concerning your life in the future, your purpose, and your destiny.

I don't think there would be any reasonable person who wouldn't be interested in knowing what God has to say about their future. This is all the more true today because people are spending more and more money consulting psychic readers, horoscopes, numerology, and all sorts of astrological means in an attempt to appease themselves and know what their future will be.

In this book, we will discuss the following topics relating to future events:

- The Reliability of the Bible
- The Rapture
- The Tribulation Period
- The Millennial Kingdom
- The Eternal State
- How Do I Fit into the Plan of God?

The study of biblical prophecy or future events is a very interesting and important study for every person. When you know what God's plans are for you in the future, it will immensely affect the way you live your life now. It will also help you see that to begin to prepare for the future means surrendering your life to the Lord Jesus. This study has opened my own spiritual insights into the significance of God's plan.

I present this book with the purpose of glorifying God, praying that this will convince anyone who has not placed their faith in the Lord Jesus Christ that He is their only means of entrance into heaven, and their escape from eternal punishment. It is also my desire that it will drive believers to live a renewed and devoted life to God.

Joe Philip

ONE

THE RELIABILITY OF THE BIBLE

The Bible is not an ordinary book, for it is God's message or instruction to mankind, whom He has created and loves unconditionally. If God being who He is has a message that He would like to communicate to His creatures, shouldn't we at least give it our attention? Yet what we find too often is that we are so busy with minor concerns like what to wear or what to eat for lunch or dinner. There is a place for these concerns but not at the expense of neglecting our God who created all things and died to save us. If the President of the United States has a message for you, wouldn't you drop everything you were doing and quickly try to find out what it is? You would show such earnestness because of who he is and the implications of what he has to say to you. Now think of God who is infinitely more superior than the President of the United States. How much more earnestly should your response be to what God has to say to you? Have you taken any effort to find out what your Creator has to say to you?

That is why the Bible is a book of infinite value and should be taken very seriously. It contains the message that can transform your life instantly and set your eternal destiny. Moreover, it can change your life for the better from the inside out and grant you such peace and fulfillment in your life like you have never experienced. *"For the word of God is quick, and powerful, and sharper than any twoedged sword, piercing even to the dividing asunder of soul and spirit, and of the joints and marrow, and is a discerner of the thoughts and intents of the heart"* (Heb. 4:12). But it has to begin with your willingness to read it and embrace its life-changing message. Won't you consider reading the all time best-seller in the world?

The truth is that we cannot know or understand Christ, the Saviour of mankind apart from the Bible, which is God's Word. Well, you may be thinking, "How can we trust it to be God's Word, when there are several other religious books that claim the same?" It is only reasonable for you to think that way. Can we prove that the Bible is the Word of God? The answer is "yes". In this chapter, I would like to present several evidences to reasonably trust the Bible to be God's Word. Whether you choose to believe that the Bible is God's Word or not, it doesn't change the fact that it is God's Word. I would encourage you to objectively examine the Bible and determine the outcome of your investigation. But if it is indeed God's Word, are you willing to believe it and obey it?

Please consider with me the following reasons why you should trust the Bible to be God's Word:

1. **The Bible itself claims that it's God's Word.** *"All scripture is given by inspiration of God, and is profitable for doctrine, for reproof, for correction, for instruction in righteousness: That the man of God may be perfect, thoroughly furnished unto all good works"* (2 Tim. 3:16-17). This may not suffice the rational skeptic who is not satisfied with merely looking at the claims that the Bible makes concerning itself. It is not sufficient to accept a religious book as God's Word strictly based on its self-proclaimed authority as the revelation of God. Yet it does add value to its own claim as God's Word. Since the Bible explicitly claims to be the exclusive revelation of God to man, we evaluate it based on objective evidences.

   There could also be people who say that the Bible is the result of human imaginations or fables. If it was man's word, I would not dare believe anything it has to say. But the reality is that there is a vast amount of evidence that it is indeed God's Word written as people were inspired by the Spirit of God by way of revelation. *"For the prophecy came not in old time by the will of man: but holy men of God spake as they were moved by the Holy Ghost"* (2 Pet. 1:21). When the Apostle Paul was writing to the church at Corinth, he wanted them to realize that what he was writing to them were not his own ideas or suggestions, but the commandments of the Lord. *"What? came the word of God out from you? or came it unto you only? If any man think himself to be a prophet, or spiritual, let him acknowledge that the things that I write unto you are the commandments of the Lord"* (1 Cor. 14:36-37).

2. **There are over 3,000 occurrences in the Old Testament of the phrases "God said", "the word of the Lord" and "the Lord spoke".** These phrases establish the fact that over 3,000 instances are recorded in the Bible where God directly spoke His mind concerning various issues to godly people. One of such occurrence is when God spoke to Noah after the flood instructing him to step out of the ark. *"And God spake unto Noah, saying, Go forth of the ark, thou, and thy wife, and thy sons, and thy sons' wives with thee"* (Gen. 8:15-16).

    The Bible also refers to God specifically speaking to prophets in communicating His message and ultimately through His Son Jesus. *"God, who at sundry times and in divers manners spake in time past unto the fathers by the prophets, Hath in these last days spoken unto us by his Son, whom he hath appointed heir of all things, by whom also he made the worlds"* (Heb. 1:1-2). The climax of God's revelation to man is in the person of Christ. Over 2,000 years ago, Jesus Christ —the Son of God came into this world by assuming human flesh in order to communicate the love of God to a lost world of sinners.

3. **There are over 200 specific prophecies about Christ in the Old Testament, written around 400 – 1450 years before the birth of Christ that have been fulfilled with**

100% accuracy. Prophecies in the Bible are predictions that are made by prophets under the inspiration of God far in advance of its fulfillment. There are strict guidelines in the Bible when it comes to prophecy. *"But the prophet, which shall presume to speak a word in my name, which I have not commanded him to speak, or that shall speak in the name of other gods, even that prophet shall die. And if thou say in thine heart, How shall we know the word which the Lord hath not spoken? When a prophet speaketh in the name of the Lord, if the thing follow not, nor come to pass, that is the thing which the Lord hath not spoken, but the prophet hath spoken it presumptuously: thou shalt not be afraid of him"* (Deut. 18:20-22). These prophecies are not vague or ambiguous, but explicit in its predictions. They are required to communicate to people exactly what was communicated to them by God. There is no exception or deviation from this standard and the violators of this law were stoned to death.

The following are a few of the fulfilled prophecies concerning the Lord Jesus that were made anywhere from 500 to 1,000 years prior to His birth:

EVENT	OLD TESTAMENT PROPHECY	NEW TESTAMENT FULFILLMENT
The birthplace of Jesus: Bethlehem	Micah 5:2	Matthew 2:1-2
The manner of Jesus' birth: born of a virgin	Isaiah 7:14	Luke 1:26-27 Matthew 1:22-23
Live in Galilee	Isaiah 9:1	Matthew 2:22
Sold for thirty pieces of silver. Potter's field bought with the betrayal money	Zechariah 11:12-13	Matthew 26:14-16 Matthew 27:5-7

EVENT	OLD TESTAMENT PROPHECY	NEW TESTAMENT FULFILLMENT
The manner of Jesus' death: pierced and hanged on a tree	Zechariah 12:10 Psalm 22:16	John 19:34
None of His bones were broken	Psalm 34:20	John 19:36
Soldiers cast lots for His coats	Psalm 22:18	Matthew 27:35
The resurrection of Jesus	Psalm 16:10	Matthew 28:5-6

Table 1: Comparison of the Fulfilled Prophecies

"Indeed, the most stupendous miracle recorded in the Bible, the resurrection of Jesus Christ, has been authenticated by numerous scholarly studies including the late great Dr. Simon Greenleaf. Dr. Greenleaf was the Royal Professor of Legal Evidences at Harvard University. He was goaded by his students into looking at the evidences for the resurrection. After a thorough examination he came back and said, 'There is not a single unbiased juror in the world who would ever look at the evidence and deny it.' Dr. Simon Greenleaf became a Christian. The Bible is not mythology and was never meant to be read as such."[1]

4. **There are numerous archeological sites that have been excavated in the 19th and 20th century that provide evidence to Biblical places, civilizations, wars, and people.** A Jewish archaeologist said, "It may be stated categorically that no archaeological discovery has ever contradicted a biblical reference."[2]

---

1   www.equip.org
2   www.godandscience.org/apologetics/bibletru.html

Let us look at a couple of examples of the historical accuracy of the Bible. Dr. Bryant Wood, a leading archeologist on Jericho, after the site where the walls of Jericho once stood had been explored and studied concluded that the walls of Jericho did not simply disintegrated over time but collapsed completely as a result of a massive attack. Their findings agree conclusively with the biblical account of what happened to the walls of Jericho as described in Joshua 6. *"So the people shouted when the priests blew with the trumpets: and it came to pass, when the people heard the sound of the trumpet, and the people shouted with a great shout, that the wall fell down flat, so that the people went up into the city, every man straight before him, and they took the city"* (Josh. 6:20).

Another example is the biblical account in Genesis 14 of how Abraham defeated Chedorlaomer king of Elam and the five kings who were with him. Critics have discredited this account of the Bible as being untrue because they didn't believe these kingdoms existed during the time of Abraham.

5. **The historicity of Jesus.** There are extra biblical references to Jesus by historians like Flavius Josephus, a first century historian. He wrote of Jesus: "So he [Ananus, son of Ananus the high priest] assembled the Sanhedrin of judges, and brought before him the brother of Jesus, who was called Christ, whose name was James, and some others (or some of his companions) and when he had formed an accusation against them, he delivered them to be stoned."[3]

6. **The preservation of the Bible down through the centuries.** If the Bible is God's message to mankind, then it is equally important to preserve it and make it accessible to the common people. The Bible is a book that is 3,500 years old and written by over 40 authors that lived in different geographical locations over a

---

3   Flavius Josephus, The Antiquities of the Jews, 20.9.1

time span of 1,500 years. What an amazing book! It is not easy to maintain the accuracy of this book when the autographs (original manuscripts) are non-existent. So, what we currently have are hand written copies of the original manuscripts. In an era where there were no computers, memory devices, nor printing machines that could store the data reliably, how did they validate the accurate transmission of the Bible?

In the Jewish community there were dedicated men who were scribes (Masoretes) who basically copied letter for letter and verified the integrity of the new copy with the old by counting the number of letters in the new copy with the ones in the old copy. The earliest of the Masoretic manuscripts available dated around 800 A.D. Another set of scribes from the Qumran community had manuscripts dating back to the time of Jesus. These manuscripts were discovered in 1947 near the Dead Sea and hence called the Dead Sea Scrolls (DSS). It "has yielded about 40,000 fragments of 400 different mss. [manuscripts], 100 of which are biblical, representing every OT [Old Testament] book except Esther. Remarkably, a comparison of the DSS and the Masoretic text reveals a fairly small number of discrepancies. Thus the ms. [manuscript] evidence for the OT firmly demonstrates that the original OT texts were carefully preserved and are accurately represented in our modern Bible."[4]

"There are tens of thousands of manuscripts from the New Testament, in part or in whole, dating from the second century A.D. to the late 15th century, when the printing press was invented."[5]

7. **The uniformity of the Bible is exceptional and mind-boggling even though it was written by over 40 authors that lived in different geographical locations**

---

4   www.4truth.net/fourtruthpbbible.
5   www.godandscience.org/apologetics/bibleorg.html

over a time span of 1,500 years. The Bible is divided into two major sections, namely, the Old Testament and the New Testament. The Old Testament contains 39 books written during 1450 and 400 B.C. Whereas, the New Testament contains 27 books written during 45 and 95 A.D.

Many of the authors lived in diverse cultural, social, and economical backgrounds. Not only that, the Bible is diverse in its literary style, for it contains, poetry, historical accounts, prophesies, allegories, word-pictures, symbols, types, shadows, moral laws, spiritual truths, and biographies. In order to fully understand the significance of such a diverse pool of authors converging into a central message without contradicting one another, we will have to consider the following scenario: Imagine that you're tasked to compile a book that is to be written by over a dozen independent authors focusing on a single topic. Once they are finished you will be totally surprised with the amount of disunity among the authors on that very topic. If that's true of topics relating to humanities, then imagine the diversity that should be found in the Bible ranging from simple topics and issues on morality to complex discussions on afterlife experiences, the resurrection body, and future events in the plan of God. But what you will discover once you read the Bible is that there is tremendous unity and flow in the message contained in each book of the Bible. The central message of the Bible is the love of God in saving people who are sinners through the sacrificial death of Christ. There is only one logical answer to that and that is the authors were inspired of God, thus assuring the integrity of the message from its only source – God Himself.

8. **The Bible is the most widely translated and published book in the world.** According to a statistical study, the number of different languages and dialects

THE RELIABILITY OF THE BIBLE

in which publication of at least one book or portions of the Bible has been accomplished is 2,287. (www. biblica.com). The Bible is the best-selling book of all times with a staggering 6 billion copies in the world in spite of extraordinary efforts by numerous emperors, leaders, dictators, and kings to destroy it.

9. **The transformed lives of millions around the world would attest to the validity of the claims that the Bible makes concerning the lifestyle of its followers.** There are thousands of stories of individuals who hated the Bible and would do anything to destroy its followers, yet when they believed its claims their lives were instantly transformed. Their life experiences began to correlate with the ones whose lives are described in the Bible.

"John Newton (1725-1807) sought lustful pleasures throughout his early life. He was also a man of extreme violence and was a ruthless slave-trader. However, this man who victimized men and women himself became a victim. His life collapsed as he himself was sold into slavery. In the midst of his despair he called out to Jesus for salvation. Once saved, his life was totally transformed. After his conversion, he was ordained to the ministry. Today, we do not remember John Newton as one of the vilest men who ever lived. Instead, we remember him as the man who penned the words, "Amazing grace, how sweet the sound that saved a wretch like me. I once was lost, but now am found; was blind, but now I see".[6]

If the Bible is not God's Word and does not have the power it claims it has to transform lives, then how can you explain the conversion of John Newton and thousands of lives that have been changed instantly by simply reading a verse or so of the Bible?

---

6   www.instituteofbiblicaldefense.com/1997/05/transformed-lives/

10. **The list of martyrs for Christ will give a sense of how dearly they loved and obeyed the Bible and followed the Lord Jesus.** Polycarp was a follower of the Lord Jesus and lived between 70 and 155 A.D. serving as a bishop in the church at Smyrna, he was a direct student of the Apostle John, who was a disciple that the Lord Jesus had personally called and commissioned. Due to the increased persecution of the Roman emperors against Christians during this period, Polycarp was arrested for being a Christian. "Amidst an angry mob, the Roman proconsul took pity on such a gentle old man and urged Polycarp to proclaim, 'Caesar is Lord'. If only Polycarp would make this declaration and offer a small pinch of incense to Caesar's statue he would escape torture and death. To this Polycarp responded, 'Eighty-six years I have served Christ, and He never did me any wrong. How can I blaspheme my King who saved me?' Steadfast in his stand for Christ, Polycarp refused to compromise his beliefs, and thus, was burned alive at the stake".[7]

The story of Polycarp is significant because it happened within the first century when the New Testament was just completed. If the historical accounts contained in the New Testament, especially the four gospels and the church history recorded in the book of Acts by Luke were false, can you imagine what the fate of its writers and its followers from the public would have been? The New Testament would have been completely rejected by the Jewish people. There would have been none to follow its teachings. Instead what we see in the first century is an unprecedented transformation of lives that did not occur over the course of many years, but instantly, within a day or so, thousands of lives were changed and became followers of the Lord Jesus. These followers were willing to be martyrs in

---

7   www.polycarp.net

order to uphold its truths and way of life. This kind of devotion and commitment by ordinary people to a book can only be explained in light of what they truly believed about the Bible and its authenticity as God's Word and its transforming power.

What I have listed above are only a few evidences and reasons why you should consider reading the time-tested book, the Bible. It has been read, studied, and followed by millions around the world. Its message is still appealing to thousands regardless of their social, economical, or religious background. What that suggests is that this is a book that offers solutions to the heart of our complex problems, addresses our innermost desires and longings to know God in a personal way. In light of such overwhelming evidences, supporting the Bible as God's Word to mankind, what will you do with the Bible? Will you consider reading it and submitting to its truths? If you do, I assure you that you will not regret it and your life will be amazingly transformed.

TWO

THE RAPTURE

The world seems to be moving forward as usual for the past thousands of years with the normal cycles of life—birth and death, societal problems—crime and violence, economic challenges—poverty and hunger, global threats—war and atrocities, natural calamities—earthquakes and floods, and so on. If this is the typical course of human history from the time of its inception, why would anyone think there is going to be a major world event that would significantly change the future of this world forever? I wouldn't believe that for a moment, if it was not for the Lord Jesus Christ who, being the upholder of this world, had promised that He would come back and gather His people (the church) unto Himself. This process of gathering His people unto Himself is referred to as the "rapture". The next major event that will take place at any moment is the rapture of the church, the reason being that there is nothing impeding its fulfillment according to the Bible. It is for this glorious event that the church has been waiting patiently and expectantly, serving faithfully, and living sacrificially ever since its conception.

IS THE RAPTURE A BIBLICAL TRUTH?

Even though the word "rapture" does not occur in the Bible, yet the truth is taught in the Bible. It is common for biblical scholars to coin terms that would describe a truth or event in the Bible for easy referencing and understanding. "Rapture" is another one of those terms. The word "rapture" is a Latin word meaning "caught up". The process of being "caught up" describes the manner in which the Lord is going to snatch His people out of this world to His home in heaven to be with Him forever. *"Then we which are alive and remain shall be caught up together with them in the clouds, to meet the Lord in the air: and so shall we ever be with the Lord"* (1 Thess. 4:17).

The rapture is a biblical truth because it is absolutely based on the promise of the Lord Jesus to His disciples. *"In my Father's house are many mansions: if it were not so, I would have told you. I go to prepare a place for you. And if I go and prepare a place for you, I will come again, and receive you unto myself; that where I am, there ye may be also"* (John 14:2-3). When the disciples of Jesus came to know from their Master that He was returning to heaven, they were deeply distressed and saddened. They really trusted Him and depended on Him for everything. They wished that they could spend the rest of their lives with Him. The news of His departure came as a shock and it caused them to really think about how they were going to face the struggles of life in His absence.

Once you have come to know the Lord Jesus as your personal Saviour and Lord, it is unthinkable to live life without Him. And that is how His disciples felt at that moment. In order to comfort their hearts, the Lord revealed this wonderful promise, that their Master and Lord will come again and gather His people unto Himself to be with Him in heaven forever. Then there will be no more separation. Even if there were no other references to the rapture in the Bible, this one promise of the Lord is sufficient for us to believe.

MAJOR EVENTS INCLUDED IN THIS TIME PERIOD – SEVEN YEARS

From the time the rapture of the church occurs, there will be a period of seven years that will catastrophically change life in this world of ours. During this seven year period there is going to be three major events in heaven (where the Lord's people will be after the rapture) and four major events on earth (where the unsaved will be after the rapture). For the Lord's people it will be a time of exuberant joy and eternal rest, whereas for unbelievers, it will be a time of unprecedented judgment and devastation unlike anything they have ever suffered before in their lives. In this chapter we shall consider the three major events taking place in heaven.

a. The rapture marks the inauguration of this glorious period for the Lord's people.
b. The Judgment Seat of Christ
c. The Marriage of the Lamb

TWO PHASES OF CHRIST'S SECOND COMING

A close study of biblical prophecy (a truth that is recorded in the Bible years in advance of its fulfillment) reveals that there are two-phases for the second coming of Christ, which are separated by a period of seven years. The first phase of Christ's second coming is the rapture, which puts into motion the impending plan of God until the eternal state. The second phase of Christ's second coming is the glorious appearing of Christ visibly on the earth to rightfully claim it as His own and to set up His kingdom for a period of a thousand years. If the rapture will be a private event with His own people, then the glorious appearing will be a public event with the unsaved people who are living at that point in time. "*And then shall appear the sign of the Son of man in heaven: and then shall all the tribes of the earth mourn, and they shall see the Son of man coming in the clouds of heaven with power and great glory*" (Matt. 24:30). In the glorious appearing of Christ, the world will see Him with power and great glory.

a. Rapture – 1st phase of Christ's second coming
b. Glorious appearing – 2nd phase of Christ's second coming

THE RAPTURE

When will the rapture occur?

Throughout history, men have tried to set dates as to when the rapture will occur. Unfortunately, every one of them has proved to be wrong. Can we really pinpoint a date for Christ's coming? Absolutely not! This was something that His disciples were very curious to know. Right before He was leaving this world, they asked Him, saying, *"Lord, wilt thou at this time restore again the kingdom to Israel? And he said unto them, It is not for you to know the times or the seasons, which the Father hath put in his own power"* (Acts 1:6-7). This is something that the Father has chosen not to reveal to His people. Most likely, to keep us waiting expectantly at all times for His coming. Yet the Bible reveals that it can occur at any moment, for nothing is dependant on its fulfillment. From a prophetic standpoint, there is nothing that really holds Him back from coming at any moment. *"Behold, I shew you a mystery; We shall not all sleep, but we shall all be changed, In a moment, in the twinkling of an eye, at the last trump: for the trumpet shall sound, and the dead shall be raised incorruptible, and we shall be changed"* (1 Cor. 15:51-52). If you don't know the day or the hour of His coming, how much more should you be certain of your salvation and the assurance that you will be raptured at His coming? If you are uncertain about your relationship with Christ, don't let another moment go by without believing and confessing Him as your Saviour and Lord.

Who will be raptured?

What is referred to as "His people" in the beginning of this chapter is a general term that encompasses two groups of people separated by two covenants that God made with mankind, namely, the Old Testament saints and the New Testament saints who comprise the church.

> **The church** – that includes every born-again (the act of God that causes a person to be born into the family of God upon his or her repentance of sin and confession of faith in Christ) child of God since the establishment of the church until the rapture, who has accepted Christ as his or her personal Saviour and Lord. If Christ were to come now, what will happen to

those believers who have died? Will they miss the rapture? Is the rapture only for those who are alive at His coming? The Apostle Paul addressed these questions that were raised by the first century believers in his letters to the Corinthian assembly. First we shall deal with those who are alive. *"Behold, I shew you a mystery; We shall not all sleep, but we shall all be changed"* (1 Cor. 15:51). The Apostle Paul had an interesting way of alluding to the death of a believer in Christ as being "asleep". Here Paul is revealing a mystery (a truth that cannot be understood by mankind until it has been revealed by God and one that has not been revealed until now) concerning believers in Christ, that all of them will not die, but a remnant will remain alive at the coming of Christ to gather His people to heaven. Now concerning those who are dead in Christ, they shall be raised at the coming of Christ, which we will discuss later in this chapter.

The Old Testament saints – that includes every person prior to the establishment of the church, who believed in God through faith based on God's revelation. These would include godly people like Abel, Noah, Abraham, David, and so on. *"And these all, having obtained a good report through faith, received not the promise: God having provided some better thing for us, that they without us should not be made perfect"* (Heb. 11:39-40). The writer alludes to the fact that these godly men and women lived their lives in accordance to God's revelation, but did not receive the promise yet, which is perfection. God does not want to make them perfect apart from us, rather together. Even though we may be God's people, as long as we live in our present bodies in this fallen world, we are imperfect. We will only be made perfect by God at His coming, when we shall possess glorified bodies.

Moreover, there are only two headships (representing two groups of people) – Adam and Christ. *"For as in*

Adam all die, even so in Christ shall all be made alive. But every man in his own order: Christ the firstfruits; afterward they that are Christ's at his coming" (1 Cor. 15:22-23). In Adam we are who we are by nature, sinners and rebels of God, whereas, in Christ we are born-again, righteous and lovers of God. The Old Testament saints cannot be in Adam because then they will be lost (for "in Adam all die"). The alternative is that they are in Christ, which shall make them alive at His coming. For example, Moses who was the lawgiver of the Old Testament is spoken of as suffering "the reproaches of Christ" in regard to his earthly sufferings, which suggests that Moses suffered what we presently suffer for the sake of Christ. Whether in the Old Testament period or the New Testament period, there is only one way to God, and that is through Christ. *"Esteeming the reproach of Christ greater riches than the treasures in Egypt: for he had respect unto the recompence of the reward"* (Heb. 11:26). If the Old Testament saints suffered for Christ's sake (even though they might not have explicitly understood as we now do) wouldn't they be also included in the gathering of His people to heaven?

What will happen during the rapture?

The amount of information that the Bible provides regarding the rapture is tremendous, which makes it an established truth based solely on God's revelation and not on man's ideas. The Apostle Paul says,

> *But I would not have you to be ignorant, brethren, concerning them which are asleep, that ye sorrow not, even as others which have no hope. For if we believe that Jesus died and rose again, even so them also which sleep in Jesus will God bring with him. For this we say unto you by the word of the Lord, that we which are alive and remain unto the coming of the Lord shall not prevent them which*

are asleep. For the Lord himself shall descend from heaven with a shout, with the voice of the archangel, and with the trump of God: and the dead in Christ shall rise first: Then we which are alive and remain shall be caught up together with them in the clouds, to meet the Lord in the air: and so shall we ever be with the Lord.

1 Thessalonians 4:13-17

It is important to note that in the Bible there are two types of resurrections, which again correlates with the two groups of people that exists in the world, namely, the saved and the unsaved. Do you know which group you belong to? It is absolutely critical to know where you stand in relation to Jesus because that will determine your future, not only for the short term but for all of eternity. Don't let this matter go unsettled, but make it certain this very moment. Jesus said, *"Marvel not at this: for the hour is coming, in the which all that are in the graves shall hear his voice, And shall come forth; they that have done good, unto the resurrection of life; and they that have done evil, unto the resurrection of damnation"* (John 5:28-29). The first type of resurrection is called the *"resurrection of life"* referring to the resurrection of the saved who are dead. The second type of resurrection is called the *"resurrection of damnation"* referring to the resurrection of the unsaved who are dead. If you are not part of the resurrection of life, you are heading toward eternal condemnation, and at that point there is no recourse. If you want to be part of the resurrection of life—repent of your sins and believe in Christ right now.

The resurrection of life is further subdivided into sections. The first phase of the resurrection of life will occur during the rapture when all the dead who are saved will be raised. The second phase of the resurrection of life will occur after seven years from the rapture until the closure of the Great Tribulation, which culminates at the glorious appearing of Christ when all the tribulation saints who became martyrs during the Tribulation Period will be raised.

The Apostle Paul lays down clearly the order of events associated with the rapture. Even though there are several intermediate events, it is an instantaneous event that takes place in a moment, in the twinkling of an eye. One mathematician has calculated an estimated speed of blinking an eye at 1 trillionth of a second. That is so quick we cannot even comprehend it! Yet that is how quickly the rapture will occur. It just tells me how awesome and mighty God is!

The following are the order of events associated with the rapture:

1. The Lord Jesus who is presently seated at the right hand of God in heaven will descend from heaven with a shout.
2. The voice of an archangel will sound.
3. The trumpet of God will sound.
4. The dead in Christ will rise first with glorified bodies.
5. First-phase of the first resurrection (resurrection of all those who are dead in Christ up until the time of rapture).
6. The living believers will be changed to possess glorified bodies.
7. Both the dead and the living will be caught up together in the clouds.
8. We shall meet the Lord in the air.
9. We shall always be with the Lord from then on.

THE JUDGMENT SEAT OF CHRIST

The next event that will occur after the rapture of the saved is the judgment seat of Christ. According to the Romans, the judgment seat or "bema" is a raised platform where the ruler sat to make decisions and pass sentences. This is not to be confused with the Great White Throne judgment where the unsaved will be judged to eternal condemnation. The judgment seat of Christ is not an event where the Lord will punish the saved for their sins; rather it is an event where rewards will be given depending on how one has used his or her life for the Lord. It will be an award ceremony hosted by the Lord Jesus for His disciples.

Its purpose

To recognize and reward the believers by their Master and Lord Jesus Christ for faithfully serving Him from the time of their conversion until death or the rapture, whichever comes first. The Apostle Paul says, *"For we must all appear before the judgment seat of Christ; that every one may receive the things done in his body, according to that he hath done, whether it be good or bad"* (2 Cor. 5:10). The Lord is going to recognize each of His servants as to what they did with their lives, whether good or bad. Can you imagine what a splendid moment that will be when the King of kings will recognize you by name in the host of angelic beings and the saints of all ages? *"For the Son of man shall come in the glory of his Father with his angels; and then he shall reward every man according to his works"* (Matt. 16:27). As the disciples of Christ, we should be looking forward to His coming because He is coming to honour us and recognize us. *"Therefore, my beloved brethren, be ye stedfast, unmoveable, always abounding in the work of the Lord, forasmuch as ye know that your labour is not in vain in the Lord"* (1 Cor. 15:58). If you want to receive rewards on that day, now is the time to act and live according to His will.

Its recipients

Every believer in Christ. It will not be a recognition based on your church, your fellowship group, your Bible study group, your prayer group, your organization, or any other such associations. It will be strictly based on your faithfulness to the Lord. The thrilling aspect of this reward is that it is not limited to the prayer warriors, the giants in faith, the pioneer workers, and the great teachers of the Bible, but is available to every believer in Christ no matter how simple or insignificant their task might be. Everyone will be rewarded fairly and justly by our Master.

Its rewards

The Scripture describes rewards in terms of crowns. These crowns may be literal crowns or the perfect ability to enjoy these special recognitions. Whatever the case may be, since it's awarded by the Supreme person, it has to be exceptional, unparalleled, glorious, and magnificent. It will be perfectly fulfilling. Moreover, it will recompense all our present sacrifices that we willingly endure for the sake of Christ. The following are the five crowns that are mentioned in the Scriptures that believers would be rewarded with for faithfully serving the Lord during their lifetime.

1. The Imperishable Crown – For those who subdued the old nature (lived overcoming sin and temptations) (1 Cor. 9:24-25).

2. The Crown of Righteousness – For those who have fought the good fight, finished the race, and kept the faith. Also for those who love His appearing. (2 Tim. 4:6-8).

3. The Crown of Life – For those who endured trials and afflictions without complaining for the sake of Christ (James 1:12).

4. The Crown of Glory – For those who faithfully served as overseers among the flock of God (1 Pet. 5:2-4).

5. The Crown of Rejoicing – For those who won souls for Christ (1 Thess. 2:19-20).

Its Responsibilities

The Scripture teaches that the Lord will assign us future responsibilities in the kingdom of God based on our faithfulness to the spiritual gifts He has bestowed upon us presently. The parable of the talents illustrates this truth. *"His lord said unto him, Well done, thou good and faithful servant: thou hast been faithful over a few things, I will make thee ruler over many things: enter thou into the joy of thy lord."* (Matt. 25:21). How we handle our present responsibilities will determine our future responsibilities in the kingdom of God. Whatever gifts the Lord has blessed you with, use it faithfully, and it will translate into greater responsibilities in the kingdom of God. A solemn thought that should stir our hearts to deeper commitment and faithfulness to the Lord.

Its process

To determine whether a believer's work deserves reward or not. The twofold process that the Lord will utilize to determine the quality of a person's work are fire and light. The Lord will not require assistance from anyone to evaluate the work of His servants, for He is Omniscient (all knowing). He has the ability to analyze our hearts to determine the intents and motives of our actions. There is no need for anyone to doubt His judgments because He will be just and perfect in all His judgments. *"For true and righteous are his judgments"* (Rev. 19:2).

1. **The believer's work will be tested by fire to determine what sort it is** – whether it will endure or whether it will be burned. If it endures, he will be rewarded accordingly, whereas if it is burned, he will suffer loss. *"Now if any man build upon this foundation gold, silver, precious stones, wood, hay, stubble; Every man's work shall be made manifest: for the day shall declare it, because it shall be revealed by fire; and the fire shall try every man's work of what sort it is. If any man's work abide which he hath built thereupon, he shall receive a reward. If any man's work shall be burned, he shall suffer loss: but he himself shall be saved; yet so as by fire"* (1 Cor. 3:12-15).

    If our work has to endure the test of fire, it has to be built with enduring materials like gold, silver, and precious stones. Our work has to bring glory to God and edify others in order for it to be of an enduring nature. All other work that falls short of these essential requirements will be burned and that believer will suffer loss, regretting not faithfully laboring for the Lord. What sort of work is yours?

2. **The believer's work will be tested by light to determine the motives of his work.** The Lord's standards are absolutely righteous and anything that falls short of this will not be worthy of praise from the Master. *"...he that judgeth me is the Lord. Therefore judge nothing before the time, until the Lord come, who both will bring to light the hidden things of darkness, and will make manifest the counsels of the hearts: and then shall every man have praise of God"* (1 Cor. 4:4-5).

The Lord is not merely interested in what we do, but also why we do it. It is one thing that we may not understand as we look at another person's ministry. In order to reveal the motives of our action, which are now hidden to others, yet manifested clearly by the light of His glory on that day. Anything that was done for self-will or self-glory will not be praiseworthy, whereas, everything that was done according to the Lord's will and for the glory of God will be praised by the Master. It is wise not to pass our judgment on other's work, until the Lord comes because He will judge accurately. Whose praise do you value the most – man's or God's? If you're interested in human praise, you will work according to human standards. But if you're interested in God's praise, you will work according to God's standard.

THE MARRIAGE SUPPER OF THE LAMB

The marriage supper of the Lamb will be the next major event after the judgment seat of Christ for the redeemed in heaven. Marriage is a solemn and momentous occasion in any culture. Imagine what a splendid occasion the marriage of the Lamb will be. There has never been or ever will be a marriage like this, for this is the marriage of the King of kings and Lord of lords. The love story behind this marriage is too wonderful for our finite minds to even comprehend. Let me try to give you a concise and simple account of this love story.

In order to find a bride for the Son of God, the heavenly Father sent His Son to this fallen world, to seek out a bride that is mortal and sinful, and in no way a comparable partner for the eternal Son of God who is infinitely holy and righteous. Yet His unconditional love of infinite proportion made His eyes fixed on us. He took on human flesh, thereby totally transforming His living conditions, for the greatest sacrifice of all. In order to win His bride's heart, He had to willingly endure and die the most horrific and painful death to save us sinners from eternal condemnation. After all this, He was willing to bless us with all spiritual blessings in the heavenly places and make us, who were created from the dust of the ground, co-heirs of all His inheritance, which is basically everything in the universe. Finally before He left the world, He promised that He would return and take His bride home to heaven, where they will be together forever. What an amazing love story! Do you know that He did all this for you? How can you not fall in love with such a wonderful person? If you haven't opened your heart to Him, accept Him today.

What an appropriate moment for the ultimate marriage of the universe, following the believers recognition and rewards by the Lord for all of their service. Perhaps, even more than the church, the Lord is excited about this exquisite and glorious moment, when He will be given a spotless and holy bride - the church- by His Father. This is an expression of the Father's eternal love for the Son. This will be the consummation of the relationship between the church and the Lord and they will forever be united in an inseparable relationship. Are you preparing yourself to meet your Bridegroom? Will the Lord be pleased with your life?

Who is the Bridegroom?

The Bridegroom is the Lord Jesus. It would only be appropriate to talk a little about the Bridegroom, for He is the ultimate Bridegroom. Here is what the Father had to say about His own Son, *"This is my beloved Son, in whom I am well pleased"* (Matt. 3:17). Here is what the Bible had to say about the Lord

Jesus, *"Who is the image of the invisible God, the firstborn of every creature: For by him were all things created, that are in heaven, and that are in earth, visible and invisible, whether they be thrones, or dominions, or principalities, or powers: all things were created by him, and for him: And he is before all things, and by him all things consist. And he is the head of the body, the church: who is the beginning, the firstborn from the dead; that in all things he might have the preeminence. For it pleased the Father that in him should all fulness dwell; And, having made peace through the blood of his cross, by him to reconcile all things unto himself; by him, I say, whether they be things in earth, or things in heaven"* (Col. 1:15-20). Truly, He is the perfect Bridegroom that every bride would desire to be married to. He desires to have a relationship with you, but are you willing to have Him in your life?

Who is the bride?

The bride is the church (consisting of all believers in Christ from the day of Pentecost until the rapture). *"Husbands, love your wives, even as Christ also loved the church, and gave himself for it...This is a great mystery: but I speak concerning Christ and the church"* (Eph. 5:25, 32). Let us look at what the Bible had to say about the bride's past. *"And you hath he quickened, who were dead in trespasses and sins; Wherein in time past ye walked according to the course of this world, according to the prince of the power of the air, the spirit that now worketh in the children of disobedience: Among whom also we all had our conversation in times past in the lusts of our flesh, fulfilling the desires of the flesh and of the mind; and were by nature the children of wrath, even as others"* (Eph. 2:1-3). Basically we are totally unworthy to be Christ's bride, but He cleansed us from all of our sins with His precious blood.

Here is what the Lord Jesus has done and is doing for us to make us the perfect bride. *"...even as Christ also loved the church, and gave himself for it; That he might sanctify and cleanse it with the washing of water by the word, That he might present it to himself a glorious church, not having spot, or wrinkle, or any such thing; but that it should be holy and without blemish"* (Eph. 5:25-27). We were not qualified to be His bride, yet He made us qualified through His glorious work of redemption on the cross.

Who are the invited guests?

Most likely, the invited guests are the Old Testament saints like Abel, Noah, Abraham, David, the prophets, and the priests, who lived faithfully for the Lord. The Old Testament saints are referred to as "the friend of the bridegroom." *"Ye yourselves bear me witness, that I said, I am not the Christ, but that I am sent before him. He that hath the bride is the bridegroom: but the friend of the bridegroom, which standeth and heareth him, rejoiceth greatly because of the bridegroom's voice: this my joy therefore is fulfilled"* (John 3:28-29). *"Abraham believed God, and it was imputed unto him for righteousness: and he was called the Friend of God"* (Jas. 2:23). Even though they were not given the privilege to be the bride of Christ, yet the Lord has called them as His own people. Another guest that will be present will be the angelic host, who had been present for all the major events of God ever since their creation. The marriage will take place in the presence of this glorious audience. All of heaven is preparing for this grand event. Are you preparing yourself to meet the Lord?

The Consummation of the Marriage

The consummation of the marriage not in the physical sense, but in the spiritual sense will take place after the judgment seat of Christ and prior to the Lord's second coming. It will be an exclusive event, only for the heavenly audience to witness. Since Christ's bride is always spoken of as "heavenly" (it is unlikely that the marriage would take place on earth). *"For our conversation is in heaven; from whence also we look for the Saviour, the Lord Jesus Christ"* (Phil. 3:20). As New Testament believers we belong to heaven because we have been redeemed out of this world. *"And I heard as it were the voice of a great multitude, and as the voice of many waters, and as the voice of mighty thunderings, saying, Alleluia: for the Lord God omnipotent reigneth. Let us be glad and rejoice, and give honour to him: for the marriage of the Lamb is come, and his wife hath made herself ready. And to her was granted that she should be arrayed in fine linen, clean and white: for the fine linen is the righteousness of saints"* (Rev. 19:6-8). Once we are glorified at the time of the rapture and the rewards have been given, we are made ready for the marriage, having no spot or wrinkle. Once we have been made ready there is no need to wait for the marriage. *"That he might present it to himself a glorious church, not having spot, or wrinkle, or any such thing; but that it should be holy and without blemish"* (Eph. 5:27).

PRESENT DAY IMPLICATIONS

1. Are you looking forward to the Lord's coming?
2. Are you engaged in the work that the Lord has assigned you to do?
3. Will you receive rewards or suffer loss?
4. What are you building with for the Lord's work – perishable things or imperishable things?
5. Are you living a holy life in preparation for the marriage supper of the Lamb?

DECISIONS

Write down the decisions that you made in light of this chapter.

_____

_____

_____

_____

_____

_____

THREE

THE TRIBULATION PERIOD

Immediately following the rapture of the church, and simultaneously with the events that will take place in heaven, will be a period of great judgment upon the wicked nations and the nation of Israel. This seven year period can be divided into two phases called "the Tribulation" and "the Great Tribulation". While those who are saved are in heaven with the Lord Jesus, enjoying the glories of heaven in perfect peace and harmony, the unsaved (who have rejected Christ) and the wicked nations will suffer great pain and destruction on earth. This is not to be confused with the eternal condemnation of the unsaved in the lake of fire, but a time of God's judgment upon the living. In this chapter we will discuss the four major events that will occur on this earth during the Tribulation Period.

MAJOR EVENTS DURING THIS TIME PERIOD – SEVEN YEARS

There are four major events that will simultaneously occur on the earth that will forever change the course of this world. Even though the world has suffered great losses, undergone severe judgments of God, endured natural calamities, yet there has never been a time of destruction on the earth like it will be during the seven years of tribulation. The following are the four major events:

1. The Period of Tribulation
2. The Period of Great Tribulation
3. The Battle of Armageddon
4. The Second Phase of Christ's Second Coming

MAJOR RULERS DURING THE TRIBULATION PERIOD – (SOME OF THESE NAMES MIGHT REPRESENT THE SAME PERSON)

1. The Antichrist (the beast out of the sea) (Rev. 13:1-8, 1 John 2:18)
2. The False Prophet (the beast out of the earth) (Rev. 13:11-17)
3. The Dragon / Satan / devil / the serpent of old (Rev. 12:9)
4. The kings of the East (Rev. 16:12)
5. The man of sin / the son of perdition (2 Thess. 2:3)
6. The one who comes in his own name (John 5:43)
7. The little horn (Dan. 7:8)
8. The king of fierce features (Dan. 8:23-25)
9. The prince who is to come (Dan. 9:26)
10. The willful king (Dan. 11:36)
11. The worthless shepherd (Zech. 11:17)
12. The scarlet beast with seven heads and ten horns (Rev. 17:4, 8-14)
13. The king of the North (Dan. 11:6)
14. The king of the South (Dan. 11:40)
15. The Russian alliance (Ezek. 38:2-39:11)

THE PERIOD OF TRIBULATION

Its Duration

The seven years of tribulation is divided into two phases: the Tribulation, which is the first phase, lasts for 3½ years; the Great Tribulation, which is the second phase, lasts for 3½ years. The first half of the Tribulation Period will be milder in judgment in comparison to the second half.

Let no man deceive you by any means: for that day shall not come, except there come a falling away first, and that man of sin be revealed, the son of perdition; Who opposeth and exalteth himself above all that is called God, or that is worshipped; so that he as God sitteth in the temple of God, shewing himself that he is God. Remember ye not, that, when I was yet with you, I told you these things? And now ye know what withholdeth that he might be revealed in his time. For the mystery of iniquity doth already work: only he who now letteth will let, until he be taken out of the way. And then shall that Wicked be revealed, whom the Lord shall consume with the spirit of his mouth, and shall destroy with the brightness of his coming: Even him, whose coming is after the working of Satan with all power and signs and lying wonders, And with all deceivableness of unrighteousness in them that perish; because they received not the love of the truth, that they might be saved. And for this cause God shall send them strong delusion, that they should believe a lie: That they all might be damned who believed not the truth, but had pleasure in unrighteousness.

2 Thessalonians 2:3-12

The Events During the Tribulation Period

During the Tribulation period, there will be changes in economic, social, political, and religious spheres all across the world. A major player who will come into the world's political scene as its spokesman would be the Antichrist. He will emerge as the peacemaker and will sign peace accords with Israel and other nations. As things move peacefully on earth, God begins to intervene directly in the lives of the people by executing His wrath upon wicked sinners. It would be foolish to think that the world will continue as it always has been with God who seems to be silent to the atrocities and violence

41

that are taking place. The God of the Bible is a just and holy God who will bring justice to every evil that has taken place in the world. The world will then realize that God does exist as the Bible demonstrates. The judgment of God will begin with the opening of the "seals". As each seal is opened, the judgment of God will fall upon the world, causing great calamities and loss of lives.

In addition to the judgments of God, there will be unprecedented events that will take the world in surprise, even though future events of this world have been revealed in the Word of God well in advance . Some of the events listed below are not in the order of its execution, but a summary of what will take place in the future.

1. **A covenant will be signed between Israel and the head of the revived Roman Empire.** This will mark the beginning of the Tribulation Period and the prophetic clock will begin to start as far as God's dealings with Israel is concerned, which really ended with the crucifixion of Christ their Messiah. *"And he shall confirm the covenant with many for one week"* (Dan. 9:27). The meaning of "one week" is seven years and is explained in detail in the chapter – "70 weeks". The revived Roman Empire comprises of the countries that made up the Roman Empire, which could be comprised of the present day European Union. Presently there are 27 countries in the European Union, namely, Belgium, France, Germany, Italy, Luxembourg, Netherlands, Austria, Bulgaria, Cyprus, Czech Republic, Denmark, Estonia, Finland, Greece, Hungary, Ireland, Latvia, Lithuania, Malta, Poland, Portugal, Romania, Slovakia, Slovenia, Spain, Sweden, and United Kingdom.

    The signing of this covenant will be of historic proportion since no leader has been able to influence Israel to maintain peace with its neighbours. It will also guarantee Israel's protection and the right to build their temple, which has been destroyed from the time of

Roman Emperor Titus in 70 A.D. The signing of this covenant will bring recognition and praise to the head of the revived Roman Empire. From this point onwards, things will move rapidly as God begins to intervene in such a way that everyone alive will experience the effects of God's dealings firsthand. Even the atheist will know that God exists and is a living and powerful influence in their lives.

2. **The opening of the seals commences the judgments of God upon the wicked.** This is when there will be visible destruction on this earth of untold proportions. As I write of the awful destruction that awaits this world, I take no pleasure in it, but pray that everyone reading this book would come to Christ in repentance and believe in Jesus Christ as their personal Saviour and Lord, thereby avoiding the judgments described in the Bible. Do not doubt for a moment as to whether or not these judgments will be fulfilled precisely the way it is described in the Bible. God "who cannot lie" has revealed these things beforehand, so that, we can heed His warnings and avoid the terrible judgment that He is going to bring upon this world (Titus. 1:2).

   a. **First seal is opened** – (Rev. 6:1-2). Most likely, it is the Antichrist who is pictured as the conqueror. In the initial stages of the Tribulation Period, the Antichrist seems to be a peacemaker (symbolized by the white horse that he rides upon) and has the upper hand on what's happening in the world. *"And I saw, and behold a white horse: and he that sat on him had a bow; and a crown was given unto him: and he went forth conquering, and to conquer."*

   Notice the overwhelming attention and rewards that he will receive as he comes to the world stage because of his good deeds and popularity. It is quite possible for the Antichrist to be alive today, but he himself won't know and the world won't know until it is God's time to reveal him and the church is taken out of this world by the Lord Jesus.

b. **Second seal is opened** – (Rev. 6:3-4). When the second seal is opened people will start killing one another—the start of worldwide violence and murder. Today, the world is plagued with violence and murder, but when the second seal is opened, it will be the beginning of mass violence and murder like the world has never seen. *"And when he had opened the second seal, I heard the second beast say, Come and see. And there went out another horse that was red: and power was given to him that sat thereon to take peace from the earth, and that they should kill one another: and there was given unto him a great sword."*

Even though now we complain about violence and the lack of peace around the world, there is coming a time when peace will be removed and what remains will be the escalation of violence and of murder of one another. Can you imagine what will be going through the minds of people as they step out of their homes to engage in daily business during this time period?

c. **Third seal is opened** – (Rev. 6:5-6). When the third seal is opened, there will be worldwide famine and shortage of goods. The world has gone through several famines that have caused tremendous damage to the world population. But when the third seal is opened, it will affect the world economy and drive the prices of goods to an all time high. The world will experience the ultimate depression and people will die due to starvation. *"And when he had opened the third seal, I heard the third beast say, Come and see. And I beheld, and lo a black horse; and he that sat on him had a pair of balances in his hand. And I heard a voice in the midst of the four beasts say, A measure of wheat for a penny, and* *three measures of barley for a penny; and see thou hurt not the oil and the wine."*

d. **Fourth seal is opened** – (Rev. 6:7-8). When the fourth seal is opened, one-fourth of the world's population will be killed due to murder, famine, and attacks of beasts. *"And when he had opened the fourth seal, I heard the voice of the fourth beast say, Come and see. And I looked, and behold a pale horse: and his name that sat on him was Death, and Hell followed with him. And power was given unto them over the fourth part of the earth, to kill with sword, and with hunger, and with death, and with the beasts of the earth."*

If the tribulation were to occur now, approximately 1.75 billion people (out of 7 billion) would vanish due to murder, famine, and the attacks of the beasts. No catastrophe has ever taken so many lives. Can you imagine what it would be like to live in the midst of such dangers and sorrow?

e. **Fifth seal is opened** – (Rev. 6:9-11). When the fifth seal is opened, the world will see the first martyrs of the Tribulation Period, those who believed the message of the kingdom and did not receive the mark of the beast. *"And when he had opened the fifth seal, I saw under the altar the souls of them that were slain for the word of God, and for the testimony which they held: And they cried with a loud voice, saying, How long, O Lord, holy and true, dost thou not judge and avenge our blood on them that dwell on the earth? And white robes were given unto every one of them; and it was said unto them, that they should rest yet for a little season, until their fellowservants also and their brethren, that should be killed as they were, should be fulfilled."*

They are killed for their obedience to the Word of God and for their faithful testimony. Now you may not have to give your life for your faith in

Christ, but during the Tribulation Period, those who believe in Christ could be killed.

f. **Sixth seal is opened** – (Rev. 6:12-17). When the sixth seal is opened, there will be natural and cosmic destruction. Nature becomes violent, earthquakes erupt, the sun is darkened, the moon becomes as blood, stars fall from the sky to earth, heaven is rolled back like a scroll, mountains and islands move out of their place. *"And I beheld when he had opened the sixth seal, and, lo, there was a great earthquake; and the sun became black as sackcloth of hair, and the moon became as blood; And the stars of heaven fell unto the earth, even as a fig tree casteth her untimely figs, when she is shaken of a mighty wind. And the heaven departed as a scroll when it is rolled together; and every mountain and island were moved out of their places. And the kings of the earth, and the great men, and the rich men, and the chief captains, and the mighty men, and every bondman, and every free man, hid themselves in the dens and in the rocks of the mountains; And said to the mountains and rocks, Fall on us, and hide us from the face of him that sitteth on the throne, and from the wrath of the Lamb: For the great day of his wrath is come; and who shall be able to stand"*

No matter who they may be—kings or subjects, great men or common people, rich or poor, free or slave, these natural and cosmic destructions will fall upon them indiscriminately. They will desire and wish that the mountains and rocks will fall on them so as to hide themselves from the wrath and the face of the Lord Jesus Christ. It just shows us the magnitude of the judgment of God that will fall upon the wicked. Do you have the assurance that you will not come under the judgment of God? You can have the absolute assurance, right now, if you come to God in repentance and believe in Jesus Christ for your deliverance from the judgment of God.

3. **While the judgment of God takes place upon this earth, God has a plan to save as many people as possible from destruction.** In order to save those who would turn to God in repentance during the period of Tribulation and fulfill God's plan, 144,000 Jews (12,000 per the tribes of Israel) will be sovereignly saved, sealed, and sent throughout the world to preach the gospel of the kingdom (Rev. 8:1-8). *"And this gospel of the kingdom shall be preached in all the world for a witness unto all nations; and then shall the end come"* (Matt. 24:14).

They will be the messengers and the missionaries of Jesus Christ during the Tribulation Period like the believers of present day, taking the gospel of the kingdom to the four corners of the world. There will be a massive conversion of souls to Christ during this period. If you, for a moment, think that the God of the Bible is an unjust and a blood thirsty God, look at His compassion for lost sinners, even in the midst of judgment, He has a plan in place to save as many people as He can from eternal punishment.

4. **A major player that Satan will equip and use during the Tribulation Period is the Antichrist.** The Antichrist ("beast out of the sea") will be revealed, and he will come to power, not by waging war as a dictator, but through deception that he is the Messiah and the Saviour (Rev. 13:1-8). In the midst of such destruction and hopelessness, people will be looking for a "god-like" figure who will act as their saviour. He will deceive the people by his charm and peace-making abilities. He will receive his abilities and power directly from Satan.

5. **Another player that Satan will equip and use during the Tribulation Period is the False Prophet** ("beast

coming out of the earth"). He would probably be a Jew and a leader of Israel. His objective will be to convince the people to believe in the Antichrist through Satanic deception by performing miracles, wonders, and raising the Antichrist. (Rev. 13:11-17). It is also suggested by biblical scholars that the false prophet could be the Antichrist and the beast out of the sea could be simply the head of the revived Roman Empire. Either way, they will both be against Christ and Satan's envoys.

6. **Since mankind has always been religious, it would be foolish on the part of Satan to totally ignore the religious aspect of this deception.** Therefore, the world-wide religious organization will be setup, which is referred to as "Babylon the Great". It will declare itself to be of God, in contrast to the true church or the bride of Christ, that is raptured in the air. *"And I saw a woman sit upon a scarlet coloured beast, full of names of blasphemy, having seven heads and ten horns. And the woman was arrayed in purple and scarlet colour, and decked with gold and precious stones and pearls, having a golden cup in her hand full of abominations and filthiness of her fornication: And upon her forehead was a name written, MYSTERY, BABYLON THE GREAT, THE MOTHER OF HARLOTS AND ABOMINATIONS OF THE EARTH"* (Rev. 17:3-5).

Today, there are so many churches springing up everywhere, but are they all part of the true church — the body of Christ? It may be difficult for us to differentiate them, but there are some that are clearly in violation of the New Testament scriptural pattern. The head of the church — the Lord Jesus Christ — will differentiate them and remove all those who are not part of the body of Christ. But if you're a church member, it would be vital to examine if you're part of the body of Christ. You can be certain by ensuring that you have repented of your sins and believed in Jesus Christ. If you are a part of the true church, check if the church that you attend is following the New Testament pattern as modeled in the Scriptures.

The events listed above were a summary of what will take place in the future during the first part of the Tribulation Period. If the first part of the Tribulation Period is God's general judgment upon the wicked, then the second part of the Tribulation Period is God's specific judgment upon the nation of Israel for their rebellion and rejection of the Messiah. This doesn't mean that the non-Jewish people will not come under the judgment of God during the second half, but that God's purpose during this period is to draw in a remnant of His own people Israel to repentance and belief in the coming Messiah.

THE PERIOD OF GREAT TRIBULATION

The Great Tribulation is the second phase of the Tribulation Period and it is referred to in the Bible as "The great day of the Lord", "a day of wrath, and "the time of Jacob's trouble". *"The great day of the Lord is near, it is near, and hasteth greatly, even the voice of the day of the Lord: the mighty man shall cry there bitterly. That day is a day of wrath, a day of trouble and distress, a day of wasteness and desolation, a day of darkness and gloominess, a day of clouds and thick darkness, A day of the trumpet and alarm against the fenced cities, and against the high towers"* (Zeph. 1:14-16).

"Alas! for that day is great, so that none is like it: it is even the time of Jacob's trouble" (Jer. 30:7).

During the great tribulation, which is the last 3½ years of the Tribulation Period, there will be continued natural calamities and loss of lives as a result of the wrath of God upon the wicked. Also, it will be a time when God will be directly dealing with His people, the nation of Israel, as He did in the past (before the conception of the church) after a long period of silence. The purpose of this intervention by

God is to cause the nation of Israel to repent in order to save the believing remnant.

The judgment of God will continue when the seventh seal is opened which will lead into seven bowl judgments and then the seven trumpet judgments. The wrath of God during this period will be intense and severe, which will culminate with the coming of the Lord in all His glory and power along with His army to destroy the armies in defiance against the Lord. While the judgment of God continues there will be major world events in the economic, social, and political fronts initiated by the Antichrist and the leaders of the major nations, driven by satanic influence and deception.

Its Duration – The Great Tribulation will last for 3½ years.

> *When ye therefore shall see the abomination of desolation, spoken of by Daniel the prophet, stand in the holy place, (whoso readeth, let him understand:) Then let them which be in Judaea flee into the mountains: Let him which is on the housetop not come down to take any thing out of his house: Neither let him which is in the field return back to take his clothes. And woe unto them that are with child, and to them that give suck in those days! But pray ye that your flight be not in the winter, neither on the sabbath day: For then shall be great tribulation, such as was not since the beginning of the world to this time, no, nor ever shall be. And except those days should be shortened, there should no flesh be saved: but for the elect's sake those days shall be shortened. Then if any man shall say unto you, Lo, here is Christ, or there; believe it not. For there shall arise false Christs, and false prophets, and shall shew great signs and wonders; insomuch that, if it were possible, they shall deceive the very elect. Behold, I have told you before. Wherefore if they shall say unto you, Behold, he is in the desert; go not forth: behold,*

he is in the secret chambers; believe it not. For as the lightning cometh out of the east, and shineth even unto the west; so shall also the coming of the Son of man be. For wheresoever the carcase is, there will the eagles be gathered together. Matthew 24:15-28

If the Great Tribulation were to continue there wouldn't be anyone alive. Such will be the magnitude of God's fierce judgment upon evildoers. The reason the Great Tribulation will be as short as it will be is for the sake of God's elect, Israel. Due to God's mercy and grace upon the elect, He will shorten the days of tribulation. No one can withstand the judgment of God.

A question that many raise today is, "How can a good and benevolent God allow suffering and pain to continue and come upon people?" There is absolutely no change to the essential character of God's goodness, what He has been from eternity past, He will be forever. But the reason God doesn't act now upon every evil action as you might think He should is because He has appointed a time when He will thoroughly and completely deal with evil and its doers. The Tribulation Period is a time when God deals directly with the evil present on the earth.

Events During the Great Tribulation

1. **The Antichrist will become more influential and powerful in the world scene during the Great Tribulation because the dragon, Satan, gives him power and he is elected by the ten-nation revived Roman Empire as its head.** *"...the dragon gave him his power, and his seat, and great authority"* (Rev. 13:2). It is Satan who will give him his power, his throne, and authority. *"And the ten horns which thou sawest are ten kings, which have received no kingdom as yet; but receive power as kings one hour with the beast. These have one mind, and shall give their power and strength unto the beast"* (Rev. 17:12-13). This ten-nation revived Roman Empire will receive authority and soon they will

transfer their power and authority to the Antichrist. *"And it was given unto him to make war with the saints, and to overcome them: and power was given him over all kindreds, and tongues, and nations"* (Rev. 13:7). The Antichrist will make war against God's people and he will overcome them since they will die rather than submit to him and his requirements. His authority will be global. With the present globalization initiatives, it is not difficult to visualize a leader who will have worldwide authority.

2. **In order to regulate global commerce and economy by the Antichrist, a scheme called "the mark of the beast" will be implemented worldwide.** This will give the Antichrist unlimited access and extensive power worldwide over the economy, for without it, he will not be able to exercise global authority. *"And he causeth all, both small and great, rich and poor, free and bond, to receive a mark in their right hand, or in their foreheads: And that no man might buy or sell, save he that had the mark, or the name of the beast, or the number of his name"* (Rev. 13:16-17). The present credit card system is a precursor to the worldwide identification system that will be required to generate a cash free economy. "Sweden was the first European country to introduce bank notes in 1661. Now it's come farther than most on the path toward getting rid of them…In most Swedish cities, public buses don't accept cash; tickets are prepaid or purchased with a cell phone text message. A small but growing number of businesses only take cards, and some bank offices — which make money on electronic transactions — have stopped handling cash altogether."[8] "The decline of cash is noticeable even in houses of worship, like the Carl Gustaf Church

---

8   http://www.washingtonpost.com/world/europe/high-tech-sweden-edges-closer-to-becoming-cashless-society/2012/03/17/gIQANtd2HS_story.html

in Karlshamn, southern Sweden, where Vicar Johan Tyrberg recently installed a card reader to make it easier for worshippers to make offerings."

Moreover, scientists now have the technology to implant microchips into our body that can store vital personal identification information. This technology has advanced to where a person that has this microchip implanted can be tracked globally, engage in vital financial transactions, and serve as government issued IDs.[9] "In announcing VeriPay to ID World delegates, Silverman stated the implant has "enormous marketplace potential" and invited banking and credit companies to partner with VeriChip Corporation (a subsidiary of ADS) in developing specific commercial applications beginning with pilot programs and market tests...Applied Digital's announcement in Paris suggested wireless technologies, RFID development, new software solutions, smart-card applications and sub dermal implants might one day merge as the ultimate solution for a world fraught with identity theft, threatened by terrorism, buffeted by cash-strapped governments and law-enforcement agencies looking for easy data-collection, and corporations interested in the marketing bonanza that cutting-edge identification, payment, and location-based technologies can afford."

3. **The current movement to harmonize world religions and faiths will consolidate into an organization** that will have significant influences in the lives of people during the Tribulation Period. It is referred to as "Babylon the Great" and will be hated and destroyed by the Antichrist because it has a "Christian" impression and is in the way of him attaining supremacy in the world. It will be destroyed in accordance to the will of God. Even though the Antichrist is under the influence of Satan and devoted to the fulfillment of his

---

9   http://www.wnd.com/2003/11/21944/

plans, yet the Lord is sovereign and has the ability to put thoughts into his heart to fulfill His purposes. *"And the ten horns which thou sawest upon the beast, these shall hate the whore, and shall make her desolate and naked, and shall eat her flesh, and burn her with fire. For God hath put in their hearts to fulfil his will, and to agree, and give their kingdom unto the beast, until the words of God shall be fulfilled. And the woman which thou sawest is that great city, which reigneth over the kings of the earth"* (Rev. 17:16-18).

4. **In order to have dominance in the religious realm, the Antichrist will proclaim himself to be God.** This is not something new. Major world religions were started by people, some proclaiming themselves to be God. Unlike anyone of the past, Satan has a vested interest in having the Antichrist act as God to deceive people during the Great Tribulation Period and keep them from worshipping the true and living God. The Bible refers to this act as "abomination of desolation" where the Antichrist sets himself up in the Jewish temple as God and demands worship from all, acclaiming power in the religious realm too. *"For that day shall not come, except there come a falling away first, and that man of sin be revealed, the son of perdition; Who opposeth and exalteth himself above all that is called God, or that is worshipped; so that he as God sitteth in the temple of God, shewing himself that he is God"* (2 Thess. 2:3-4). It is interesting to note that when Satan wants someone to act as God, he doesn't choose the Antichrist to represent any other world religion than the biblical Christianity. One would wonder why? Even Satan knows that the God of the Bible is the true and living God, and the One against whom he is trying to wage war.

> *And they worshipped the dragon which gave power unto the beast: and they worshipped the beast, saying, Who is like unto the beast? who is able to make war with him? And there was*

*given unto him a mouth speaking great things
and blasphemies; and power was given unto
him to continue forty and two months. And he
opened his mouth in blasphemy against God,
to blaspheme his name, and his tabernacle, and
them that dwell in heaven...And all that dwell
upon the earth shall worship him, whose names
are not written in the book of life of the Lamb
slain from the foundation of the world.*

Revelation 13:4-6, 8

This will be the act that will surely intensify the judgment of God upon the wicked and, thereby, focusing Satan's attack on the godly remnant of Jews. There have been a few leaders through the course of history, who had the ability and personality to draw attention to themselves and have attempted to claim deity. But none will match the person that Satan will prepare and empower to occupy the seat of God in the rebuilt temple of God in Jerusalem and exalting himself as God. Notice, the dragon, Satan, is the one who will give him authority to speak blasphemies and do mighty things for forty-two months, which is the duration of the Great Tribulation. His deception will be so meticulous and calculated that everyone who dwells on the earth during the Great Tribulation will worship him except for those who fear and worship God.

5. **Since the Antichrist has to occupy the seat of God in the Jewish temple, he will have to break the covenant he made at the beginning of the Tribulation Period between Israel and the revived Roman Empire during the middle of the Tribulation Period.** From this point on, the Jews will be tormented and his true character will be manifested to the world, that he is not really a peacemaker, but the very embodiment of sin.

"…and in the midst of the week he shall cause the sacrifice and the oblation to cease" (Dan. 9:27).

The breaking of the covenant with Israel will not only have political implications, but surely spiritual as well. This means that they will not have the liberty to perform sacrifices and offerings in the temple of God. This will immensely affect their right to worship their God in their own land. The reason the Antichrist wants all sacrifices and offerings ended is so that he can now accept their worship.

6. **A war will erupt in heaven between Michael and his angels and Satan and his angels, which will result in Satan and his demons losing access to heaven and being cast down to earth, probably in preparation for the descent of the New Jerusalem.** *"And his tail drew the third part of the stars of heaven, and did cast them to the earth…And there was war in heaven: Michael and his angels fought against the dragon; and the dragon fought and his angels, And prevailed not; neither was their place found any more in heaven. And the great dragon was cast out, that old serpent, called the Devil, and Satan, which deceiveth the whole world: he was cast out into the earth, and his angels were cast out with him"* (Rev. 12:4, 7-9). Presently, Satan has access to heaven and is *"the prince of the power of the air, the spirit that now worketh in the children of disobedience"* (Eph. 2:2). But he will be stripped of his powers one by one until he has none left by the King of kings.

Heaven will rejoice over the downcast of Satan and his angels and pronounce woe to the people of the earth because Satan will then intensify his persecution of Israel. Satan has always and is presently accusing believers before God day and night whenever they fall into sin. But Christ, being our Advocate before the Father, pleads our case based on His finished work on the cross. But the moment Satan is cast down, there will be great rejoicing in heaven for he will have no more access to heaven.

> *And I heard a loud voice saying in heaven, Now is come salvation, and strength, and the kingdom of our God, and the power of his Christ: for the accuser of our brethren is cast down... Therefore rejoice, ye heavens, and ye that dwell in them. Woe to the inhabiters of the earth and of the sea! for the devil is come down unto you, having great wrath, because he knoweth that he hath but a short time. And when the dragon saw that he was cast unto the earth, he persecuted the woman which brought forth the man child."*
>
> Revelation 12:10, 12-13

This defeat will aggravate Satan and hence, he will focus his persecution on God's beloved people – Israel, which is referred to here as "the woman who gave birth to the male Child." The "male Child" is Jesus who was born through the Jewish lineage. Since Satan knows that he has a short time before him until his incarceration, he will intensify his persecution of the Jewish believing remnant.

7. **A portion of Israel will flee to the desert—a place prepared by God, for their protection against Satan where they will be fed supernaturally for 1260 days or 3½ years.** *"And the woman fled into the wilderness, where she hath a place prepared of God, that they should feed her there a thousand two hundred and threescore days"* (Rev. 12:6). God will supernaturally protect a portion of the nation of Israel from the attacks of the devil, as He has always done in the past in connection with the Israelites, as well as His children who are now living under the persecution of the devil. *"My Father, which gave them me, is greater than all; and no man is able to pluck them out of my Father's hand"*

(John 10:29). Our God is omnipotent and He knows how to protect His children.

This is not new in the history of the Jewish people to find shelter in caves and mountains during invasion. According to the Jewish historian, Josephus, Jews fled to Edom and Petra during the Babylonian invasion of Judah in 6 BC, when Jerusalem and the temple were destroyed. Later, in 70 AD, when the Romans destroyed the city and the temple, many Jews fled to the mountains along the Dead Sea and were protected there from the invading army. Since the Jews are God's chosen people, He will protect them from their enemies as He has done in the past.

8. **A believing remnant of Israel will be supernaturally carried (given two wings of a great eagle) to the desert where they will be fed for 3½ years (a time and times and half a time).** *"And to the woman were given two wings of a great eagle, that she might fly into the wilderness, into her place, where she is nourished for a time, and times, and half a time, from the face of the serpent"* (Rev. 12:14). Whatever the *"two wings of a great eagle"* might be, it will be swift and powerful to carry the believing remnant of Israel to their God appointed hideout from the serpent or the devil.

In order to defeat the plans of God, Satan will cause a great flood to destroy the believing remnant of Israel, but the earth will help them by swallowing up the flood. *"And the serpent cast out of his mouth water as a flood after the woman, that he might cause her to be carried away of the flood. And the earth helped the woman, and the earth opened her mouth, and swallowed up the flood which the dragon cast out of his mouth"* (Rev. 12:15-16). *"And I heard the man clothed in linen, which was upon the waters of the river, when he held up his right hand and his left hand unto heaven, and sware by him that liveth for ever that it shall be for a time, times, and an half; and when he shall have accomplished to scatter the power of the holy people, all these things shall be finished"* (Dan. 12:7). Even though Satan has might, he is not Almighty, so he will always be out-done by the Almighty God. Let me pause for a moment, and pose this question to you: "Whose team are you on now—Satan's or Christ's?" If you are on Satan's team, you are on the losing team and in the future you will be completely defeated. But if you are on Christ's team, you are on the winning team and one day you will be reigning in victory.

Satan will become agitated over his failures to destroy the believing remnant of Israel with the flood, so he will focus his fury on individual believers rather than on the group. *"And the dragon was wroth with the woman, and went to make war with the remnant of her seed, which keep the commandments of God, and have the testimony of Jesus Christ"* (Rev. 12:17). At this point, Satan is furious and will attack particularly the Jews who keep the commandments of God and bear the testimony of Jesus Christ. This will not be something new, but now Satan will work tirelessly with all his might to cause as much damage as possible since he knows his time is limited.

9. **There will be two witnesses of God who will prophesy for 1260 days or 3½ years, which is the full duration of the Great Tribulation.** During their assignment no one will be able to hurt them because they have power to destroy anyone with fire that proceeds out of their mouths. It is believed by biblical scholars that these two witnesses could be Elijah and Moses because of the similarity of their miracles. *"These have power to shut heaven, that it rain not in the days of their prophecy: and have power over waters to turn them to blood, and to smite the earth with all plagues, as often as they will"* (Rev. 11:6). Their primary objective is to be God's witnesses to the Israelites and prophesy

since the holy city is under the control of the Gentiles. Their prophecy might come as a warning to those who reject Christ and words of hope to those who have rejected the Antichrist as their messiah.

a. **The Antichrist will kill the two witnesses with God's permission after their assignment is completed, and their bodies shall lie in the streets of Jerusalem for 3½ days because he did not allow them to be buried, instead they were watched worldwide.** *"And when they shall have finished their testimony, the beast that ascendeth out of the bottomless pit shall make war against them, and shall overcome them, and kill them. And their dead bodies shall lie in the street of the great city, which spiritually is called Sodom and Egypt, where also our Lord was crucified. And they of the people and kindreds and tongues and nations shall see their dead bodies three days and an half, and shall not suffer their dead bodies to be put in graves"* (Rev. 11:7-9). Unlike the previous generations, now it is possible to broadcast anywhere and anything live via satellite and internet. Technology has advanced with the invention of television, mobile devices, and tablets where this prophecy can be literally fulfilled now without any difficulty. Perhaps, in the last century, this idea that their dead bodies would be seen by people of all tribes, tongues, and nations would be difficult to understand and believe. This just shows that we are living in the last days. Are you ready to meet your Creator?

b. **There will be great rejoicing all over the world because the two witnesses have been killed.** They rejoice because this is their first real victory, even though they are unaware that it will be short-lived. *"And they that dwell upon the earth shall rejoice over them, and make merry, and shall send gifts one* *to another; because these two prophets tormented them that dwelt on the earth"* (Rev. 11:10).

c. **God will quicken the dead bodies of the two witnesses after 3½ days and raise them to life and will cause them to ascend up to heaven at the shout of a great voice from heaven.** Their victory indeed was short-lived. *"And after three days and an half the spirit of life from God entered into them, and they stood upon their feet; and great fear fell upon them which saw them. And they heard a great voice from heaven saying unto them, Come up hither. And they ascended up to heaven in a cloud; and their enemies beheld them"* (Rev. 11:11-12). Can you imagine what it will be like to live through the Tribulation Period when supernatural events like these occur right before your eyes?

d. **Immediately following their ascension to heaven, there will be a great earthquake which will destroy one-tenth of the city of Jerusalem resulting in 7,000 deaths.** *"And the same hour there was a great earthquake, and the tenth part of the city fell, and in the earthquake were slain of men seven thousand: and the remnant were affrighted, and gave glory to the God of heaven"* (Rev. 11:13). This incident will cause the rest of the people who are alive to give glory to God, whether willingly or not is not mentioned.

10. **There will be three important proclamations made by three angels to every person who lives on the face of the earth during this period.** It is important for the people to adhere closely to these proclamations because it will determine whether or not they will come under God's judgment. The God of the Bible is fair and just in all His judgments. He will provide adequate warnings before He executes His wrath upon those who will disobey Him.

a. The everlasting gospel will be preached by an angel to everyone who dwells on the earth during the Tribulation Period. *"And I saw another angel fly in the midst of heaven, having the everlasting gospel to preach unto them that dwell on the earth, and to every nation, and kindred, and tongue, and people, Saying with a loud voice, Fear God, and give glory to him; for the hour of his judgment is come: and worship him that made heaven, and earth, and the sea, and the fountains of waters"* (Rev. 14:6-7).

Our God is merciful and loving and desires every nation, tribe, tongue, and people to turn from the worship of the beast to the worship of God, in preparation for the coming kingdom of Christ. The everlasting gospel is what the Lord alluded to in His teachings: *"And this gospel of the kingdom shall be preached in all the world for a witness unto all nations; and then shall the end come"* (Matt. 24:14). If people fall under God's judgment, it will be only because of their rejection of the everlasting gospel.

What is the difference between the everlasting gospel and the gospel of Jesus Christ? Essentially, it is the same, for there is only one gospel, which is based on the finished work of Christ on the cross, over 2,000 years ago. Presently, we are saved by faith in Jesus Christ, but during the Great Tribulation, the emphasis will be on rejecting the worship of the beast and turning to God in preparation of the coming kingdom of Christ upon the earth. Have you placed your faith in Jesus Christ for your eternal salvation?

b. The destruction of "Babylon the Great" is declared by another angel. This proclamation is significant to know because many have put their trust in the apostate church and false religions. *"And there followed another angel, saying, Babylon is fallen, is fallen, that great city, because she made all nations drink of the wine of the wrath of her fornication"* (Rev. 14:8). This will lead some of those who are following the apostate church or a false religion for the salvation of their souls to turn from it to worship the true and living God.

At the end, there will be only one true church—the body of Christ made up of all true believers, one true way to heaven—Jesus Christ, one true method for the salvation of your soul—faith in Jesus Christ, one true Judge before whom all the unsaved living and the dead will have to appear one day for judgment—the Lord Jesus Christ, one true eternal destiny for all sinners saved by God's grace—heaven, and one true eternal destiny for all of the unsaved—eternity in the lake of fire. The choice is yours. Where will you spend your eternity, in heaven or hell?

c. **A warning against accepting the mark of the beast will be proclaimed by a third angel.** This is another warning that needs to be adhered to closely because it will determine whether or not you will come under God's judgment.

> *And the third angel followed them, saying with a loud voice, If any man worship the beast and his image, and receive his mark in his forehead, or in his hand, The same shall drink of the wine of the wrath of God, which is poured out without mixture into the cup of his indignation; and he shall be tormented with fire and brimstone in the presence of the holy angels, and in the presence of the Lamb: And the smoke of their torment ascendeth up for ever and ever: and they have no rest day nor night, who worship the beast and his image, and whosoever receiveth the mark of his name.* Revelation 14:9-11

Without the mark of the beast, it will be virtually impossible to live during the Tribulation Period. It will be required to make any purchasing or selling transactions. Anyone who will not receive the mark of the beast will have only a short time to live before they will be killed for their rejection of the beast. But that will guarantee freedom from God's judgment during the Tribulation Period and the judgment that is going to come in eternity forever. Anyone who receives the mark of the beast will be completely aware of the consequences of their choice. Presently, people reject Christ fully knowing that their action will result in them spending eternity in hell. Whatever it is that is hindering you from accepting Christ into your life, may I suggest that it is not worth eternal punishment.

11. **Continuation of the opening of the seals.** When the Lord Jesus will open the seventh seal, seven angels will be given seven trumpets to be blown, and at the sound of each trumpet, God's wrath will fall upon wicked sinners. The judgments of God during the Great Tribulation will be severe and continue to escalate in severity. The following are the seven trumpet judgments of God:

a. **Seventh seal is opened**—There was silence in heaven for half an hour and the Lord was ministering at the altar of incense, which had the prayers of the tribulation saints requesting the destruction of the enemy.

> *And when he had opened the seventh seal, there was silence in heaven about the space of half an hour. And I saw the seven angels which stood before God; and to them were given seven trumpets. And another angel came and stood at the altar, having a golden censer; and there was*

given unto him much incense, that he should offer it with the prayers of all saints upon the golden altar which was before the throne. And the smoke of the incense, which came with the prayers of the saints, ascended up before God out of the angel's hand. And the angel took the censer, and filled it with fire of the altar, and cast it into the earth: and there were voices, and thunderings, and lightnings, and an earthquake. And the seven angels which had the seven trumpets prepared themselves to sound.

Revelation 8:1-6

First Angel / Trumpet – God's wrath on nature— one-third of the trees will be burned up due to hail and fire, mixed with blood. The severity of this wrath caused all the grass to burn up. Can you imagine the devastation of fire and smoke? *"The first angel sounded, and there followed hail and fire mingled with blood, and they were cast upon the earth: and the third part of trees was burnt up, and all green grass was burnt up"* (Rev. 8:7).

Second Angel / Trumpet – God's wrath on nature will continue when a third of the sea becomes blood, a third of all the sea life vanishes, and a third of the ships are destroyed. These are catastrophic events that the world has never witnessed. *"And the second angel sounded, and as it were a great mountain burning with fire was cast into the sea: and the third part of the sea became blood; And the third part of the creatures which were in the sea, and had life, died; and the third part of the ships were destroyed"* (Rev. 8:8-9).

Third Angel / Trumpet – God's wrath on nature continues when a great star falls from the sky as a fiery ball on a third of the rivers causing the

65

destruction of lives. *"And the third angel sounded, and there fell a great star from heaven, burning as it were a lamp, and it fell upon the third part of the rivers, and upon the fountains of waters; And the name of the star is called Wormwood: and the third part of the waters became wormwood; and many men died of the waters, because they were made bitter"* (Rev. 8:10-11). People are amused and thrilled by Sci-Fi movies that portray the destruction of stars, yet when it really happens they will be surprised and devastated.

Fourth Angel / Trumpet – God's wrath on nature continues when a third of the sun will be struck, a third of the moon, and a third of the stars sustained damage causing a 33% reduction in daylight. *"And the fourth angel sounded, and the third part of the sun was smitten, and the third part of the moon, and the third part of the stars; so as the third part of them was darkened, and the day shone not for a third part of it, and the night likewise"* (Rev. 8:12).

Fifth Angel / Trumpet – When the fifth trumpet will sound, a star falls from heaven on the earth and it opens the bottomless pit which releases locusts (a composite beast) to hurt (like a scorpion) only those who do not have the seal of God. This torment will be severe and last for five months.

This particular judgment had several restrictions. The following are the restrictions:

The locusts that come out of the bottomless pit (the dwelling place of demons) will not harm the grass, any green thing, or any tree.

They are commanded to torment only those men who do not have the seal of God on their foreheads (referring to all of the unbelievers).

They were not given authority to kill them.

The pain and suffering associated with this judgment will be so intense that they will seek and desire to die, in an attempt to free themselves from this torment, but death will flee from them. Now people commit suicide to escape from life's pain and suffering. But during the Great Tribulation, even if they wanted to die, death will flee from them. In other words, there will be no escape from this suffering. Can you imagine what it would be like to live under constant torment from demons? The only reason I can think of why anyone would want to go through such agony is their utter rejection of God's love and grace and the hardness of their hearts in accepting the "angel of the bottomless pit" (could be a reference to Satan).

And the fifth angel sounded, and I saw a star fall from heaven unto the earth: and to him was given the key of the bottomless pit. And he opened the bottomless pit; and there arose a smoke out of the pit, as the smoke of a great furnace; and the sun and the air were darkened by reason of the smoke of the pit. And there came out of the smoke locusts upon the earth: and unto them was given power, as the scorpions of the earth have power. And it was commanded them that they should not hurt the grass of the earth, neither any green thing, neither any tree; but only those men which have not the seal of God in their foreheads. And to them it was given that they should not kill them, but that they should be tormented five months: and their torment was as the torment of a scorpion, when he striketh a man. And in those days shall men seek death, and shall not find it; and shall desire to die, and death shall flee from them. And the shapes of the locusts were like unto horses prepared unto battle; and on their heads were as it were crowns like gold, and their faces were as the faces of men. And they had hair as the hair of women, and their teeth were as the teeth of lions. And they had breastplates, as it were breastplates of iron; and the sound of their wings was as the sound of chariots of many horses running to battle. And they had tails like unto scorpions, and there were stings in their tails: and their power was to hurt men five months. And they had a king over them, which is the angel of the bottomless pit, whose name in the Hebrew tongue is Abaddon, but in the Greek tongue hath his name Apollyon.

Revelation 9:1-11

Sixth Angel / Trumpet – When the sixth trumpet will sound, an army of horsemen of 200 million will be on the march to kill one-third of the world population. The horse is a composite beast that has power to kill by fire, smoke, and brimstone coming out of its mouth.

One of the purposes of these judgments is to turn people from their evil ways of satanic worship, idolatry, murder, witchcraft, and immorality. Mankind has always engaged in these types of evil activities due to his sinful nature. No matter how severe the judgment of God will be, the heart of man is so wicked that they would not repent of their evil ways and turn to the living God. But presently, while God's judgment has not yet been poured out upon the wicked, there is opportunity for you to turn to God. If you're living a sinful lifestyle, it is time for you to repent of your ways and turn to Christ before it's too late. *"The heart is deceitful above all things, and desperately wicked: who can know it?"* (Jer. 17:9). Ever since the fall of man in the Garden of Eden, man has increased in wickedness and it will culminate during the Great Tribulation, when there will be an ultimate display of every kind of evil imaginable.

And the sixth angel sounded, and I heard a voice from the four horns of the golden altar which is before God, Saying to the sixth angel which had the trumpet, Loose the four angels which are bound in the great river Euphrates. And the four angels were loosed, which were prepared for an hour, and a day, and a month, and a year, for to slay the third part of men. And the number of the army of the horsemen were two hundred thousand thousand: and I heard the number of them. And thus I saw the horses in the vision, and them that sat on them, having breastplates of fire, and of jacinth, and brimstone: and the heads of the horses were as the heads of lions; and out of their mouths issued fire and smoke and brimstone. By these three was the third part of men killed, by the fire, and by the smoke, and by the brimstone, which issued out of their mouths. For their power is in their mouth, and in their tails: for their tails were like unto serpents, and had heads, and with them they do hurt. And the rest of the men which were not killed by these plagues yet repented not of the works of their hands, that they should not worship devils, and idols of gold, and silver, and brass, and stone, and of wood: which neither can see, nor hear, nor walk: Neither repented they of their murders, nor of their sorceries, nor of their fornication, nor of their thefts. Revelation 9:13-21

Seventh Angel / Trumpet – When the seventh trumpet sounds, there will be loud voices in heaven proclaiming that the Great Tribulation is coming to an end with the coming of the Lord in glory to establish His millennial kingdom on earth. God's promise to Israel is going to be fulfilled when all the kingdoms of this world have become the kingdoms of God whose king is Christ forever. Associated with this revelation will be lightening, thundering, earthquake, and great hail.

Through this proclamation, God is revealing His plans of establishing His righteous kingdom upon the earth. This is another attempt to sway people's hearts from wickedness to righteousness by believing the everlasting gospel. If only they could believe the message of God concerning the kingdom of Christ, that He is ultimately going to reign with great power on this earth forever, that He is coming to judge the wicked, that they would turn to God for salvation, that they would be spared eternal condemnation. At no point in life, is it too late to turn to God in repentance and confess Christ as Lord and Saviour.

And the seventh angel sounded; and there were great voices in heaven, saying, The kingdoms of this world are become the kingdoms of our Lord, and of his Christ; and he shall reign for ever and ever. And the four and twenty elders, which sat before God on their seats, fell upon their faces, and worshipped God, Saying, We give thee thanks, O Lord God Almighty, which art, and wast, and art to come; because thou hast taken to thee thy great power, and hast reigned. And the nations were angry, and thy wrath is come, and the time of the dead, that they should be judged, and that thou shouldest give reward unto thy servants the prophets, and to the saints, and them that fear thy name, small and great; and shouldest destroy them which destroy the earth. And the temple of God was opened in heaven, and there was seen in his temple the ark of his testament: and there were lightnings, and voices, and thunderings, and an earthquake, and great hail. Revelation 11:15-19

12. **The seven last plagues (Rev. 15-16)** The seven angels that had the seven plagues were given seven golden vials or bowls full of God's wrath to be poured out on the wicked. These seven plagues will culminate with the glorious appearing of Christ to defeat the armies arrayed against Him. *"And the seven angels came out of the temple, having the seven plagues, clothed in pure and white linen, and having their breasts girded with golden girdles. And one of the four beasts gave unto the seven angels seven golden vials full of the wrath of God, who liveth for ever and ever"* (Rev. 15:6-7).

   a. **First Bowl / Angel** – When they think that the wrath of God has been completed, then comes a new set of judgments that are more severe and intense than the previous ones. Oh! What an awful time for the those living on the earth in those days! When the first bowl is poured out, very disgusting sores break out on those who have the mark of the beast and worship his image. *"And the first went, and poured out his vial upon the earth; and there fell a noisome and grievous sore upon the men which had the mark of the beast, and upon them which worshipped his image"* (Rev. 16:2). If you recollect, God had already given them ample warning not to engage in the worship of the beast. When people simply ignore God's warnings and rebel against Him, He has no other options but to bring judgment upon them. When God engages in these judgments, He is not rejoicing over their suffering, but He does it because He is just and righteous.

   b. **Second Bowl / Angel** – When the second bowl is poured out, the sea will be turned into blood which kills every living creature. According to scientists, it is impossible to estimate how many living organisms are in the ocean, for there are many yet to be discovered. It is believed that there are over a billion living things in the ocean. This just shows the complexity of God's creation. *"And the second angel poured out his vial upon the sea; and it became as the blood of a dead man: and every living soul died in the sea"* (Rev. 16:3).

c. **Third Bowl / Angel** – When the third bowl is poured out, the rivers and springs of water become blood and are given to the people to drink. *"And the third angel poured out his vial upon the rivers and fountains of waters; and they became blood"* (Rev. 16:4). If the second bowl concentrated on the sea, then the third bowl concentrated on contaminating all of the water sources. When there is no more fresh water, it will make life virtually impossible to continue. Can you imagine the condition of people when there is not a single drop of water to be found on the earth?

God's wrath upon the wicked is just and fair because they have shed the blood of the saints and prophets of God. This judgment comes upon them as a just recompense of their own actions. If God were not to judge evil, how would justice be served for the innocent? What this reveals is not God's hatred of people, but the righteous judgments of God upon wickedness. *"And I heard the angel of the waters say, Thou art righteous, O Lord, which art, and wast, and shalt be, because thou hast judged thus. For they have shed the blood of saints and prophets, and thou hast given them blood to drink; for they are worthy"* (Rev. 16:5-6).

d. **Fourth Bowl / Angel** – When the fourth bowl is poured out, the heat of the sun is intensified causing sunburns on people. There have been hot summers in the past, when the temperature has gone over 100°F and it was extremely hot and seemed unbearable. Imagine what it will be like when the solar radiation is intensified and causes the temperature to rise to deadly levels. *"And the fourth angel poured out his vial upon the sun; and power was given unto him to scorch men with fire. And men were scorched with great heat, and blasphemed the name of God, which hath power over these plagues: and they repented not to give him glory"* (Rev. 16:8-9).

The most saddening aspect of this is that people will still be unwilling to repent and turn to God. Instead they will blaspheme the name of God. It just shows how rebellious they are with the true nature of their hearts being manifested through their hatred towards God. If Christ were to come this very moment, and you are left behind because you did not accept by faith Christ as your Lord and Saviour, then you will go through this terrible phase of the Tribulation Period and experience this firsthand. My desire and prayer is that you will repent of your sins and accept Christ into your life while it is not too late to make that decision and escape the judgment that is coming.

e. **Fifth Bowl / Angel** – When the fifth bowl is poured out, severe pain will be inflicted on the beast (Antichrist) and his kingdom with darkness for all of the wickedness that they perpetuated throughout the world. During the course of the Tribulation Period, the Antichrist and his followers will have influenced millions to worship him and receive the mark of the beast in opposition to the clear warnings of God. *"And the fifth angel poured out his vial upon the seat of the beast; and his kingdom was full of darkness; and they gnawed their* *tongues for pain, And blasphemed the God of heaven because of their pains and their sores, and repented not of their deeds"* (Rev. 16:10-11).

Like the previous judgment, which caused sinners to blaspheme the God of heaven, the Antichrist and his kingdom will blaspheme God because of the pain and suffering inflicted upon them through this judgment. They will not repent of their ways but be clearly defiant toward God.

f. **Sixth Bowl / Angel** – When the sixth bowl is poured out, the river Euphrates will be dried up miraculously to make way for the kings of the east and the whole world to gather for the battle of Armageddon. Drying up the river Euphrates will immensely help the massive movement of troops by land from the east to take their positions in and around Israel in preparation for the ultimate battle of all times, called the battle of Armageddon. This is the battle that everyone dreads but, according to the Bible, it will take place to demonstrate the supremacy of the Lord Jesus as the King. He will defeat Satan, manifesting the absolute justice of God in the midst of lawlessness, exhibiting the awesome power of God in defeating evil and evil-doers, that truth may triumph over evil in the end.

And the sixth angel poured out his vial upon the great river Euphrates; and the water thereof was dried up, that the way of the kings of the east might be prepared. And I saw three unclean spirits like frogs come out of the mouth of the dragon, and out of the mouth of the beast, and out of the mouth of the false prophet. For they are the spirits of devils, working miracles, which go forth unto the kings of the earth and of the whole world, to gather them to the battle of that great day of God Almighty. Behold,

I come as a thief. Blessed is he that watcheth, and keepeth his garments, lest he walk naked, and they see his shame. And he gathered them together into a place called in the Hebrew tongue Armageddon. Revelation 16:12-16

The influencing power that will rally the kings of the earth to gather them to the battle of that great day of God Almighty is vested in three persons, that is, the dragon or Satan, the beast or the Antichrist, and the false prophet. They will send forth spirits of demons with enormous power to perform signs and wonders that will impress these kings in pledging their allegiance to them in defeating Christ (who in their eyes is the cause of all this destruction upon the earth). The world is fed up with the pain and suffering inflicted upon them by the Lord and is seeking a resolution to this conflict. The kings of the earth are misled by these influencing powers that defeating Christ will end their misery. But for Satan, it is a battle of ideology, good versus evil, being fully aware that he himself is the defeated foe. For many people living today, Armageddon may be a fantasy, but the reality is that it will happen as the Bible describes.

It may seem that the world is a much safer place to live in, but the truth is that man's sinful nature and unregenerated heart is capable of committing the vilest crimes imaginable. The world that we presently live in will one day be the stage on which the most deadly battle that this world has ever seen will be fought. Unless the fundamental sin problem is addressed, and there is an acknowledgement of the need for a Saviour to rescue from depravity and hopelessness, and there is a willingness to turn from evil ways to God, there will not be a change in the attitude of mankind.

g. **Seventh Bowl / Angel** – When the seventh bowl is poured into the air, a great voice from the throne within the temple of heaven said, *"It is done"* (v. 17). It will be followed by voices, thunders, lightening, and earthquakes. The city of Babylon was divided into three, and the cities of the nations crumbled. Expressions like these – *"every island fled away and the mountains disappeared"* (v. 20) are difficult for our finite minds to comprehend. Yet the truth is that it will happen precisely as described in the Bible. Finally, great hail weighing a talent (100 pounds) will fall on people out of heaven. What devastation is awaiting the wicked who refuse to turn to God! My prayer is that you may not fall under God's judgment, but believe in Jesus Christ for your salvation.

> *And the seventh angel poured out his vial into the air; and there came a great voice out of the temple of heaven, from the throne, saying, It is done. And there were voices, and thunders, and lightnings; and there was a great earthquake, such as was not since men were upon the earth, so mighty an earthquake, and so great. And the great city was divided into three parts, and the cities of the nations fell: and great Babylon came in remembrance before God, to give unto her the cup of the wine of the fierceness of his wrath. And every island fled away, and the mountains were not found. And there fell upon men a great hail out of heaven, every stone about the weight of a talent: and men blasphemed God because of the plague of the hail; for the plague thereof was exceeding great.* Revelation 16:17-21

These seven bowl judgments will complete the wrath of God upon the unbelieving people of the world and usher in the glorious appearing of Christ to set up His millennial kingdom reign upon the earth as He promised to David centuries ago. In all of these judgments of God, we see God's attitude towards sin and wickedness. Even though God is love, He will not overlook sin and evil. God's attributes like love and holiness will always be exhibited in perfect harmony. These prophecies are given so that we might understand God's hatred of sin, forsake our evil ways and turn to God. During the period of Tribulation, there are no blessings, but only God's fierce wrath mingled with grace. He still gives opportunities to people to repent and turn to the living God. Don't let this moment pass by without making a decision to surrender your life to Christ.

THE BATTLE OF ARMAGEDDON

The battle of Armageddon is the battle that many people wish will not happen because of the devastation that it will inflict. The world has endured many wars and conflicts, but this battle will be one that will transform the world from what it is now to what God wants it to be. It will be the battle between Satan and his armies and Christ and `His armies, in which Christ will triumph over Satan, ushering in the kingdom of God upon the earth with Christ as its King. For the wicked, it will be a battle that they dread, but for God's people it will be a great victory over Satan and his cohorts. Even though Satan himself knows that he is a defeated foe because of the victory that Christ won on the cross over 2,000 years ago, yet the outcome of this battle will make Satan's defeat certain to the whole world.

The Duration of the Battle

As to how long this battle will last is not specified, but the underground strategies by Satan will probably begin during the early stages of the Great Tribulation and culminate at the second coming of Christ. Satan and his cohorts are no match for Christ and His army, and in that sense, the defeat will be won instantly at the appearing of Christ.

The Meaning of Armageddon

The word "Armageddon" is a Hebrew word, which means "the mountain of Megiddo". It is used only once in the Scriptures in Revelation 16:16, but this battle is referred to in other portions of the Scriptures like Matthew 24:29-31, Revelation 16:12-16, 19:11-21, and Daniel 2:31-45 without explicitly naming it. People have called it "World War III" for it will be a war in which the whole world engages.

The Major Players in this Conflict

In the Bible, when kings and kingdoms are mentioned, they are referred to in relation to a geographical location. The point of reference is always Israel. Even though many of these kings are singularly mentioned, it could be that they represent many nations who form an alliance. For example, the king of the south could represent an alliance of Arab nations under the leadership of Egypt. The following are the major players in this conflict:

1. King of the North – Assyria (Dan. 11, Zeph. 2:13)
2. King of the South – Egypt (Dan. 11)
3. Kings of the East – Federation of Oriental Nations (Rev. 16:12)
4. Russian Alliance (Ezek. 38)
5. The Revived Roman Empire under the Antichrist (Dan. 2, Rev. 19)
6. The False Prophet or the Jewish Leader (Rev. 13:11-17)
7. Dragon or Satan (Rev. 12:9)
8. The King of Kings and Lord of Lords – Lord Jesus Christ (Rev. 19)

The Antichrist is going to rally the kings of the earth with their armies to make war against Israel, and when Christ returns, he will turn their rage toward Christ and His army.

The Epicenter of the Battle

This battle is going to take place in the vast areas surrounding Israel comprising the following:

1. **The Mountain of Megiddo** (Zech. 12). The ancient city of Megiddo is located 30 km southeast of Haifa, and is located at a strategic entrance through the eastern Carmel hills. In this site an important city once existed and has been the ground where several battles have been fought in the past.

2. **The Valley of Jehoshaphat** (Joel 3). The name Jehoshaphat means "Jehovah is Judge". This valley could be between Jerusalem and the Mount of Olives, surrounding the Kidron Valley. But many biblical scholars think that this valley is yet to be formed. In that case, it would be created at the appearing of Christ and when His feet touch the Mount of Olives and it splits into two, forming a great valley.

3. **The Land of Edom** (Isa. 34:1-6, 63:1). This could be the present day geographical area of Jordan.

This campaign is going to cover the length of Israel from north to south as mentioned in Revelation 14:20, which is *"a thousand and six hundred furlongs"*. This is approximately 180 miles long.[10] Presently, the borders of Israel range from about 290 miles in length to 85 miles in width at its widest point. So, this battle is going to cover the entire land of Israel. As far as the Lord is concerned, it is a battle to reinstate the Davidic kingdom under Christ as its King. Because of this, the focus of this conflict will be on the land of Israel.

The Preparation for the Battle

This will be the greatest campaign of battles that is going to take place on the face of the earth since its creation, where

---

10   www.mfg.gov.il

there will be unprecedented death tolls and bloodshed. It is the plan of Satan to move these major players to wage war against Israel and its rightful King – the Lord Jesus Christ. The Lord Jesus will appear on the Mount of Olives and destroy those arrayed against Israel and Him.

> *Proclaim ye this among the Gentiles; Prepare war, wake up the mighty men, let all the men of war draw near; let them come up: Beat your plowshares into swords, and your pruninghooks into spears: let the weak say, I am strong. Assemble yourselves, and come, all ye heathen, and gather yourselves together round about: thither cause thy mighty ones to come down, O Lord. Let the heathen be wakened, and come up to the valley of Jehoshaphat: for there will I sit to judge all the heathen round about.*
>
> Joel 3:9-12

There will be an organized rallying of nations to prepare for this ultimate battle by the Antichrist and the major world leaders. This battle will not take them by surprise for they will be preparing for this in advance.

There will be a massive escalation in the production of sophisticated weapon systems like fighter jets, war ships, submarines, tanks, armored vehicles, nuclear weapons, and weapons of mass destruction – conventional, biological, and chemical. In order to achieve this goal, the nations of the world will allocate substantial budget towards the design, production, and implementation of these weapon systems. Where will the money come from? It will probably come from the budget allocated for other services and projects. It will not be difficult for the leaders of these nations to convince their own people that building weapon systems is their highest priority to protect them from the enemy. This is not something new; for example, during WWII, the United States geared all efforts towards building weapons. According to the U.S. Department of Defense, the defense budget for fiscal 2010 was $663.8

billion. During the Tribulation Period, defense budgets of the major nations of the world will easily exceed these figures.

Even though this battle is escalated by the Antichrist and his allies, the Lord Jesus being the Sovereign One is really the One who will be gathering these nations to fight against Israel. *"For I will gather all nations against Jerusalem to battle"* (Zech. 14:2 NIV). In other words, it will not take the Lord by surprise, for He is in absolute control of everything that is taking place on the earth during the Great Tribulation as He is with the whole universe.

The Battle Strategy

In Daniel chapter 11 and Revelation chapters 16 & 19, we get a high level strategy of how these battles will be waged, which was prophesied over 500 years prior to the birth of Christ (over 2500 years ago) by the prophet Daniel. How did Daniel know about the future? As the Bible claims, it was revealed to Daniel by the Lord. The following are the high level strategies of the battle of Armageddon:

1. **The king of the south (Egypt) shall attack the Antichrist.** *"And at the time of the end shall the king of the south push at him: and the king of the north shall come against him like a whirlwind, with chariots, and with horsemen, and with many ships; and he shall enter into the countries, and shall overflow and pass over"* (Dan. 11:40). Egypt has always been a major player in the Middle East and will continue to be until the time of the Antichrist. Events within Egypt since 2011 are shaping up to prepare it for the ultimate battle.

2. **The king of the north (Assyria) shall also attack the Antichrist with great force.** (Dan. 11:40). The Assyrians trace back their ancestry to Mesopotamia or the present day Iraq. The Assyrian empire existed as a powerful empire from 2300 BC until 600 BC. Today they are part of Iraq, Syria, Iran, and Turkey. Many of these countries have evolved politically to align with Biblical prophecy.

3. **The king of the north will invade many countries including Egypt (king of the south) and Israel.** *"He shall enter also into the glorious land, and many countries shall be overthrown: but these shall escape out of his hand, even Edom, and Moab, and the chief of the children of Ammon. He shall stretch forth his hand also upon the countries: and the land of Egypt shall not escape. But he shall have power over the treasures of gold and of silver, and over all the precious things of Egypt: and the Libyans and the Ethiopians shall be at his steps"* (Dan. 11:41-43). The Edomites, Moabites, and Ammonites have disintegrated into the regions surrounding Israel like Jordan, Syria, and Lebanon. It is probable that these nations will be subdued by a dictator who will rise to power from Iraq, Syria, Iran or Turkey. After he conquers Egypt he will have large amounts of precious resources like gold and silver, which translates into financial supremacy. He will also have dominance over the region of Libya and Ethiopia, which could mean northern Africa.

   Even though Israel will be captured by this dictator and the city of Jerusalem under his rule, yet the remnant of believing Jews will flee to the desert (Rev. 14). *"For I will gather all nations against Jerusalem to battle; and the city shall be taken, and the houses rifled, and the women ravished; and half of the city shall go forth into captivity, and the residue of the people shall not be cut off from the city"* (Zech. 14:2). Jews will be greatly persecuted and killed by this dictator.

4. **The king of the north will hear reports of masses of armies from the east and the north marching towards Israel.** *"But tidings out of the east and out of the north shall trouble him: therefore he shall go forth with great fury to destroy, and utterly to make away many"* (Dan. 11:44). This could be the kings of the east with an army of 200 million soldiers and the Russian alliance marching

towards Israel. The kings of the east could certainly include the People's Liberation Army, which has the world's largest military force, along with the nations of the Far East. The armies of the north could be marching towards the Middle East under the leadership of the Russians. Moreover, presently the relations between the Chinese and the Russians have greatly improved to the extent that they are conducting military exercises together to strengthen the Asia-Pacific region. Russian President Putin said, "We assign an important role to the joint initiative on strengthening security in the Asia-Pacific region and in this context we will maintain the relationship between our militaries."[11]

The river Euphrates will be supernaturally dried up by the Lord in order for the armies of the east to move into the Middle East and take their positions in preparation for the ultimate battle. There will be a massive movement of military vehicles and weapons from the east via land as well and so drying up the river will greatly help in this effort. "And the sixth angel poured out his vial upon the great river Euphrates; and the water thereof was dried up, that the way of the kings of the east might be prepared. And I saw three unclean spirits like frogs come out of the mouth of the dragon, and out of the mouth of the beast, and out of the mouth of the false prophet. For they are the spirits of devils, working miracles, which go forth unto the kings of the earth and of the whole world, to gather them to the battle of that great day of God Almighty. Behold, I come as a thief. Blessed is he that watcheth, and keepeth his garments, lest he walk naked, and they see his shame. And he gathered them together into a place called in the Hebrew tongue Armageddon" (Rev. 16:12-16).

5. **The king of the north will station on the mountain of Megiddo where he will be destroyed.** "And he shall plant the tabernacles of his palace between the seas in the glorious holy mountain; yet he shall come to his end, and none shall help him" (Dan. 11:45). What a sad ending!

---

11   www.news.yahoo.com

6. **The Antichrist with his ten nation army will survive to engage in battle with Israel.** *"And I saw the beast, and the kings of the earth, and their armies, gathered together to make war against him that sat on the horse, and against his army"* (Rev. 19:19).

7. **The kings of the earth and their armies will be gathered together to make war against the Lord Jesus when He will appear with His army** (Rev. 19:19).

8. **The Lord appears with His army to deliver Israel and sets His foot on the Mount of Olives, which will split in two, forming a great valley.**

> *And I saw heaven opened, and behold a white horse; and he that sat upon him was called Faithful and True, and in righteousness he doth judge and make war. His eyes were as a flame of fire, and on his head were many crowns; and he had a name written, that no man knew, but he himself. And he was clothed with a vesture dipped in blood: and his name is called The Word of God. And the armies which were in heaven followed him upon white horses, clothed in fine linen, white and clean. And out of his mouth goeth a sharp sword, that with it he should smite the nations: and he shall rule them with a rod of iron: and he treadeth the winepress of the fierceness and wrath of Almighty God. And he hath on his vesture and on his thigh a name written, KING OF KINGS, AND LORD OF LORDS*
> Revelation 19:11-16

> *Then shall the LORD go forth, and fight against those nations, as when he fought in the day of battle. And his feet shall stand in that day upon the mount of Olives, which is before Jerusalem on the east, and the mount of Olives shall cleave*

*in the midst thereof toward the east and toward
the west, and there shall be a very great valley;
and half of the moutain shall remove toward the
north, and half of it toward the south.*

Zechariah 14:3-4

9. **The Lord will destroy the armies gathered to fight
against Him.** *"And the remnant were slain with the
sword of him that sat upon the horse, which sword proceeded out of his mouth: and all the fowls were filled with
their flesh"* (Rev. 19:21). The kings of the earth will
spend an enormous amount of money, resources and
time to wage war against the Lord, but it will come
to an end virtually in no time since they will be no
match for the Lord.

What will be the outcome of the battle of Armageddon?

Today many of the enemies of Israel are calling for the
extermination of Israel and to "wipe Israel off the map". Kings
and rulers have tried to destroy the Jews in the past using
various methods, only to prove how impossible a mission it
is. According to the Bible, they are God's chosen people, who
will possess their own land and have an everlasting kingdom.
For this very reason, they will survive as a nation forever.
Abraham who is called their "father" was chosen by God
from among the nations for this very purpose. God made a
covenant with him over 4000 years ago concerning the land
that it shall be given to his descendants forever. God is faithful to keep His promises and covenants. What He has decreed
will come to pass no matter who tries to avert it.

The strategy of the One who sits on the white horse
(Christ) in defeating His enemies is twofold:

1. **The beast and the false prophet will be cast alive into
the lake of fire as its first occupants.** *"And the beast was
taken, and with him the false prophet that wrought miracles
before him, with which he deceived them that had received
the mark of the beast, and them that worshipped his image.*

These both were cast alive into a lake of fire burning with brimstone" (Rev. 19:20). This is the end of all those who go against God's plan and purpose.

2. **The rest of the army (well over a billion) will be killed with the sword that proceeds from Christ's mouth.** *"And the remnant were slain with the sword of him that sat upon the horse, which sword proceeded out of his mouth: and all the fowls were filled with their flesh"* (Rev. 19:21). Notice, their flesh will be feasted upon by the birds of the air. What a tragic ending of life!

How the Lord does this will be beyond our comprehension, but don't forget, He is the Almighty God. *"Ah Lord GOD! behold, thou hast made the heaven and the earth by thy great power and stretched out arm, and there is nothing too hard for thee"* (Jer. 32:17). Do you take the Lord seriously in your life?

The description of how the armies die from the judgment of God is chilling and gruesome. Even though they are killed with the sword that proceeds from Christ's mouth, the tremendous power of that sword is notable in the manner in which they die. "Their flesh will rot while they are still standing on their feet, their eyes will rot in their sockets, and their tongues will rot in their mouths." The sophisticated weapon systems with which they were armed are no match for the Lord Jesus.

This is the plague with which the Lord will strike all the nations that fought against Jerusalem: Their flesh will rot while they are still standing on their feet, their eyes will rot in their sockets, and their tongues will rot in their mouths. On that day people will be stricken by the Lord with great panic. They will seize each other by the hand and attack one another. Judah too will fight at Jerusalem. The wealth of all the surrounding nations will be collected—great quantities of gold and silver and clothing. A similar plague will strike the horses and

*mules, the camels and donkeys, and all the animals
in those camps.*   Zechariah 14:12-15, NIV

THE SECOND PHASE OF CHRIST'S SECOND COMING

The culmination of the battle of Armageddon happens during the second phase of Christ's second coming. There are also other events that will take place simultaneously or directly following the battle of Armageddon, which are of great significance in the plan of God. The second phase of Christ's second coming is referred to as "the appearing" because every eye will see Him as a man, yet glorified and having all authority in heaven and on earth.

The Timing of Christ's Second Coming

Even though the timing of the first phase of Christ's second coming or the rapture is not known, the second phase of His second coming is known. It will occur toward the end of the Great Tribulation or approximately seven years from the rapture (Rev. 19:11-16).

The Lord Jesus Himself predicted His second coming to His disciples while He was with them. *"Immediately after the tribulation of those days shall the sun be darkened, and the moon shall not give her light, and the stars shall fall from heaven, and the powers of the heavens shall be shaken: And then shall appear the sign of the Son of man in heaven: and then shall all the tribes of the earth mourn, and they shall see the Son of man coming in the clouds of heaven with power and great glory"* (Matt. 24:29-30).

The Old Testament prophets like Daniel and Zechariah who lived around 520 years before the birth of Christ predicted Christ's second coming, which hasn't occurred yet, but will as predicted. *"And his feet shall stand in that day upon the mount of Olives, which is before Jerusalem on the east, and the mount of Olives shall cleave in the midst thereof toward the east and toward the west, and there shall be a very great valley; and half of the mountain shall remove toward the north, and half of it toward the south"* (Zech. 14:4).

The angels of God declared Christ's second coming to His disciples during His ascension to heaven. *"And while they looked stedfastly toward heaven as he went up, behold, two men stood by them in white apparel; Which also said, Ye men of Galilee, why stand ye gazing up into heaven? this same Jesus, which is taken up from you into heaven, shall so come in like manner as ye have seen him go into heaven"* (Acts 1:10-11).

Events Associated with Christ's Second Coming

It may seem that the defeat of the Antichrist, the false prophet, and the armies of the world in the battle of Armageddon is the most important act of Christ at His second coming. But there are other equally important events that will take place at His second coming that will add to the glory and victory of Christ. The following are the events that will occur at Christ's second coming:

1. **The Second Phase of the First Resurrection**—The first phase of the first resurrection will take place at the time of rapture, which includes the church (all saved during the present age) and the Old Testament saints. *"Marvel not at this: for the hour is coming, in the which all that are in the graves shall hear his voice, And shall come forth; they that have done good, unto the resurrection of life; and they that have done evil, unto the resurrection of damnation"* (John 5:28-29).

   Then at the end of the Tribulation Period, when Christ returns to this earth, He will raise all the people who died during the Tribulation Period for their faith in Christ and for not worshipping the beast nor receiving the mark of the beast. This group of people is referred to as the Tribulation saints. *"Blessed and holy is he that hath part in the first resurrection: on such the second death hath no power, but they shall be priests of God and of Christ, and shall reign with him a thousand years"* (Rev. 20:6). This completes the first resurrection and there will be no more resurrections of life. By now, all of the saints of God from all ages will have been resurrected to life.

Those who have part in the first resurrection are blessed because they are forever freed from the power of death and they will not come under the second death, which is the eternal wrath of God in the lake of fire. Moreover, they will be priests of God and of Christ, and shall reign with Christ in His kingdom for a thousand years. Who could impart such blessings on mortal man other than God?

2. **Christ will pour the Spirit of grace and supplication out on the Jews in order to turn them to God when He comes.**

> *And I will pour upon the house of David, and upon the inhabitants of Jerusalem, the spirit of grace and of supplications: and they shall look upon me whom they have pierced, and they shall mourn for him, as one mourneth for his only son, and shall be in bitterness for him, as one that is in bitterness for his firstborn. In that day shall there be a great mourning in Jerusalem, as the mourning of Hadadrimmon in the valley of Megiddon.*   Zechariah 12:10-11

The purpose of this outpouring of the Spirit of God upon the Jews is to convict them of their sins and make them realize that the man their forefathers crucified was not a criminal, but indeed the Son of God, their Messiah, the One who had come to restore them as predicted by the prophets of old. The conviction will be so immense that they will grieve and mourn as they would for a firstborn. Their spiritual eyes will be opened by the Spirit of God to comprehend this truth. This is consistent with the working of the Spirit of God in the lives of His people even now. *"And when he is come, he will reprove the world of sin, and of right-eousness, and of judgment: Of sin, because they believe not on me"* (John 16:8-9). This supernatural work of God will yield a massive number of Jews turning to Christ as their Messiah. All of this is made possible because of the sacrifice of Christ on the cross.

God had to initiate the work of salvation because mankind is totally helpless in the sinful condition. God will put His Spirit in the lives of Jews and they shall live forever. God will raise them because they are spiritually dead to possess eternal life. *"And shall put my spirit in you, and ye shall live, and I shall place you in your own land: then shall ye know that I the Lord have spoken it, and performed it, saith the Lord"* (Ezek. 37:14). Not only will God give them eternal life, but He will restore to them their own land that God had promised Abraham his descendants would inherit forever. Once He does that, they will know that it is the Lord who has done this mighty work in their lives. At the end, God gets all the glory.

How faithful God is in keeping His promises and covenants that He made thousands of years ago to a man named Abraham! If God is faithful to keep His promises that He made with Abraham, wouldn't He be faithful to keep His covenant that He made through His own Son Jesus, that He would save all who believe in Christ from their sins. Millions of people, all around the world are standing *"In hope of eternal life, which God, that cannot lie, promised before the world began"* (Tit. 1:2). If you haven't yet trusted Jesus Christ for your salvation, won't you come to Him today? *"All that the Father giveth me shall come to me; and him that cometh to me I will in no wise cast out"* (John 6:37).

3. **At the second coming of Christ, the nation of Israel**

will be restored as God originally intended it to be.
The Israelites were scattered due to their rebellion and rejection of Christ, an ethnic group of people hated by the world because of their ties to the Messiah, and a land over which many battles have been fought. But at the second coming of Christ, Israel as a nation will be restored to its position as God's own chosen people, a nation blessed of God, and a nation ruled by its King —Christ the Lord. Then, Israel will be restored to its highest glory unlike any period in its history. *"And so all Israel shall be saved: as it is written, There shall come out of Sion the Deliverer, and shall turn away ungodliness from Jacob: For this is my covenant unto them, when I shall take away their sins"* (Rom. 11:26-27). God will do this because of His covenant with them and He will forgive them of their sins.

4. **As part of the battle of Armageddon that was discussed in detail in the previous section, the destruction of the kings of the earth and their armies by Christ with the sword that proceeded from His mouth will occur when Christ returns to earth (Rev. 19:17-20).**

5. **The capture of the beast (the Antichrist) and the false prophet by Christ and the casting of them into the lake of fire will occur as part of the battle of Armageddon when Christ returns (Rev. 19:20).** They will be the first two inhabitants of the lake of fire. They will be followed by Satan and his demons, and any unrepentant sinners at the time appointed by the Lord.

PRESENT DAY IMPLICATIONS

1. The terrible judgments of God during the Great Tribulation Period upon the wicked are a sign of God's hatred of sin.

2. Believers, we should be thankful to the Lord that we will not come under this judgment.

3. We should think twice before we commit sin.

4. If the judgment during the Great Tribulation will be so severe, then how much more was the judgment of God upon Christ when He was suffering on the cross for our sins?

5. If you haven't accepted the Lord as your personal Saviour and Lord, then do it now! You may not have another opportunity.

DECISIONS

Write down the decisions that you made in light of this chapter.

_____

_____

_____

_____

_____

_____

FOUR

THE MILLENNIAL KINGDOM

The Great Tribulation ends with the second coming of Christ with the saints and the armies of heaven to destroy nations that are arrayed against Him to wage war. This will bring closure to the Tribulation Period, which will bring an end to the awful judgments of God upon the wicked and Israel. Like any dispensation or age, there will be a transition period from the Tribulation Period to the millennial kingdom. Once the Lord judges the nations and incarcerates Satan into the bottomless pit, He will inaugurate the millennial rule of Christ on earth that has been promised to David thousands of years ago. This will mark the fulfillment of the promises and covenants that God made with Abraham and David. Unlike any previous ages since the fall of man, this age of the millennial kingdom of Christ will be the closest to perfection this fallen earth could ever experience.

MAJOR EVENTS INCLUDED
IN THIS TIME PERIOD – 1,000 YEARS

Some of the events listed below might not happen during the millennial reign of Christ, but prior to it, during the transitional period between the end of the Tribulation Period and the millennial kingdom. The judgment of the nations and the incarceration of Satan into the bottomless pit could be preparatory to the inauguration of His kingdom.

1. Judgment of the Nations (Matt. 25:31-46).
2. Incarceration of Satan into the Bottomless Pit (Rev. 20:1-3).
3. Setting Up of the Millennial Kingdom (Rev. 20:4).

4. Descending of the Holy City – New Jerusalem (Rev. 21:9-21).

5. The Final Revolt of Satan and the Nations (Rev. 20:7-10).

6. The Great White Throne Judgment (Rev. 20:11-15).

JUDGMENT OF THE NATIONS

Its Duration

The time period for the judgment of the nations is not specified, but it seems it will be a quick process following the second coming of Christ. It will probably take place after the Lord has won the battle of Armageddon.

Who is going to be judged?

All the Gentile nations, that is, all the nations except Israel, will be summoned before Christ to be judged and separated. *"And before him shall be gathered all nations: and he shall separate them one from another, as a shepherd divideth his sheep from the goats"* (Matt. 25:32). This will be a judgment of all the living at the end of the Great Tribulation. During the Tribulation Period, as a result of all the judgments of God that were poured out on the wicked, a significant population of the world has been destroyed. But there will still remain people all across the world, for whom a judgment has to be made by the Lord as to whether or not they will enter into the kingdom of Christ.

Separation of the Nations

All the Gentile nations of the world will be separated into two groups: "sheep" and "goats". *"And he shall set the sheep on his right hand, but the goats on the left"* (Matt. 25:33). This will not be a difficult task for the Judge of all because He has divine attributes that will equip Him to make this distinction quickly and easily.

Criteria for the Separation

All the Gentile nations of the world will be judged based on their treatment of the Jews (the believing remnant). *"Then shall the King say unto them on his right hand, Come, ye blessed of my Father, inherit the kingdom prepared for you from the foundation of the world: For I was an hungred, and ye gave me meat: I was thirsty, and ye gave me drink: I was a stranger, and ye took me in: Naked, and ye clothed me: I was sick, and ye visited me: I was in prison, and ye came unto me...And the King shall answer and say unto them, Verily I say unto you, Inasmuch as ye have done it unto one of the least of these my brethren, ye have done it unto me"* (Matt. 25:34-36, 40).

If they are going to be judged based on their treatment of the Jews who were persecuted during the Tribulation Period, does that mean the Lord is going to judge them based on their good deeds? The Bible is very clear on this issue. *"Therefore we conclude that a man is justified by faith without the deeds of the law"* (Rom. 3:28). No one will be granted eternal life by the Lord based on their observance of the law or by the good deeds that they have done, but solely on their faith in Christ. This is true of all ages, and the Lord is not going to make an exception for those people who will be judged at the end of the Tribulation Period.

Then, what does it mean that they will be judged based on their treatment of the Jews? The good deeds that the Lord was impressed with were *"I was thirsty, and ye gave me drink: I was a stranger, and ye took me in: Naked, and ye clothed me: I was sick, and ye visited me: I was in prison, and ye came unto me"* (Matt. 25:35-36). We are certain based on the Bible that the Lord will not judge anyone based on their good deeds, and so, the Lord points out these good deeds explicitly to prove the genuineness of their faith in Christ. Even though we are not saved by our good deeds, yet we are saved to do good deeds. *"For we are his workmanship, created in Christ Jesus unto good works, which God hath before ordained that we should walk in them"* (Eph. 2:10). These people, who treated the Jews well during the Tribulation Period, did it because of their loyalty to the Lord and their love for fellow believers. Basically, when the Lord sited these examples of good deeds, He was describing the nature of His judgment from another perspective, one that may be easily understood by mankind.

Another reason the Lord takes their treatment seriously is because whatever they did towards the Jews affected the Lord directly. The Lord said, *"Verily I say unto you, Inasmuch as ye have done it unto one of the least of these my brethren, ye have done it unto me"* (Matt. 25:40). In other words, when they fed a believing Jew who was hungry during the Tribulation Period, the Lord counted it as if He was the one being fed. What this implies is that the relationship between Christ and the believers is of such intimacy that He feels our pain and burden as well.

So, what are you depending on for the salvation of your soul? If you are depending on your good deeds, you will not enter heaven, but if you are depending solely on your faith in Christ and what He has done on the cross on your behalf, then you will be granted entrance into heaven and possess eternal life.

Destiny of the "Sheep"

All those who have treated the Jews well will be welcomed to enter the millennial kingdom and inherit eternal life. The result of their good treatment of Jews is an indication of their conversion and belief in Jesus Christ as their Lord and Saviour. *"Then shall the King say unto them on his right hand, Come, ye blessed of my Father, inherit the kingdom prepared for you from the foundation of the world…And these shall go away into everlasting punishment: but the righteous into life eternal"* (Matt. 25:34, 46).

Destiny of the "goats"

All those who have persecuted the Jews will be cast into the lake of fire to suffer everlasting punishment. The result of their bad treatment of the Jews is an indication of their lost state, their rejection of Christ, and their rejection of God's own chosen people—Israel. *"Then shall he say also unto them on the left hand, Depart from me, ye cursed, into everlasting fire, prepared for the devil and his angels…And these shall go away into everlasting punishment: but the righteous into life eternal"* (Matt. 25:41, 46).

THE INCARCERATION OF SATAN INTO THE BOTTOMLESS PIT

Satan or the devil was known as Lucifer before his fall and condemnation by God. He was created by God as the most awesome and powerful angel of God to praise Him and carry out God's missions. But sometime after Lucifer's creation, he had a desire to be like the Most High, pride took over and he tried to exalt his throne above God's. Hence God cast him out. He was stripped of his divine title and privileges. Thereafter, he became an adversary of God, trying to hinder the work of God and mislead people to commit evil. *"Be sober, be vigilant; because your adversary the devil, as a roaring lion, walketh about, seeking whom he may devour"* (1 Pet. 5:8). When Lucifer fell from his divine position as an angel of God, he caused one-third of the angels of God to rebel against God. These angels who were once God's messengers became the enemies of God and are known as demons in the Bible. Satan knows that his incarceration is very near and hence he uses all means possible to avert people from the truth.

> *How art thou fallen from heaven, O Lucifer, son of the morning! how art thou cut down to the ground, which didst weaken the nations! For thou hast said in thine heart, I will ascend into heaven, I will exalt my throne above the stars of God: I will sit also upon the mount of the congregation, in the sides of the north: I will ascend above the heights of the clouds; I will be like the most High. Yet thou shalt be brought down to hell, to the sides of the pit. They that see thee shall narrowly look upon thee, and consider thee, saying, Is this the man that made*

the earth to tremble, that did shake kingdoms; That made the world as a wilderness, and destroyed the cities thereof; that opened not the house of his prisoners? All the kings of the nations, even all of them, lie in glory, every one in his own house. But thou art cast out of thy grave like an abominable branch, and as the raiment of those that are slain, thrust through with a sword, that go down to the stones of the pit; as a carcase trodden under feet. Thou shalt not be joined with them in burial, because thou hast destroyed thy land, and slain thy people: the seed of evildoers shall never be renowned. Prepare slaughter for his children for the iniquity of their fathers; that they do not rise, nor possess the land, nor fill the face of the world with cities. Isaiah 14:12-21

Its Duration

While Christ will rule the world with righteousness, Satan will be incarcerated into the bottomless pit for 1,000 years. Satan will have no part in the kingdom of Christ and he will not influence it in any way, shape or form. From this point on, Satan will have very limited access in influencing world affairs and opportunities to engage in conflict.

Purpose of Satan's incarceration

The purpose of Satan's incarceration is to not allow Satan to deceive the nations for 1000 years and to prove to the world that God is righteous and just in all His judgments. Even without the influence or deception of Satan, people will still rebel against Christ in their hearts. *"And cast him into the bottomless pit, and shut him up, and set a seal upon him, that he should deceive the nations no more, till the thousand years should be fulfilled: and after that he must be loosed a little season"* (Rev. 20:3).

It is probable that the fallen angels could also be incarcerated with Satan for 1000 years. It would be meaningless to bind Satan for 1000 years while his cohorts are free to roam around and deceive people during the reign of Christ. Since Christ is going to reign with righteousness, He will not allow anyone to exploit His kingdom nor permit anyone to influence the subjects of His kingdom. *"For if God spared not the angels that sinned, but cast them down to hell, and delivered them into chains of darkness, to be reserved unto judgment"* (2 Pet. 2:4). *"And the angels which kept not their first estate, but left their own habitation, he hath reserved in everlasting chains under darkness unto the judgment of the great day"* (Jude 6). *"Know ye not that we shall judge angels?"* (1 Cor. 6:3).

SETTING UP OF THE MILLENNIAL KINGDOM

Its Duration
The millennial kingdom will last for 1,000 years even though Christ will be King forever. Can you imagine a single monarch ruling this world for 1,000 years?

The Kingdom and its subjects
The King who will rule during the millennial kingdom will be Christ along with His bride (the church) and the subjects of that kingdom will be the Gentile nations. The tribulation saints who did not worship the beast or his image will live and reign with Christ as well. *"And I saw thrones, and they sat upon them, and judgment was given unto them: and I saw the souls of them that were beheaded for the witness of Jesus, and for the word of God, and which had not worshipped the beast, neither his image, neither had received his mark upon their foreheads, or in their hands; and they lived and reigned with Christ a thousand years"* (Rev. 20:4).

Today, the world does not recognize nor honour the followers of Christ. Instead, they are persecuted by the enemies of the cross in many countries. But on that day, the world will recognize us and honour us because of our status as the bride of Christ. Can you imagine what it would be like to reign with Christ? The Lord is training us for reigning by allowing us to experience the trials and adversities of life. The Lord gives us responsibilities now in the spiritual realm to evaluate our faithfulness for future responsibilities in the millennial kingdom. Our future assignments and responsibilities in the millennial kingdom are going to be dependent on our present execution and faithfulness of our God-given responsibilities. Now is the time to labor for Christ tirelessly, live sacrificially, love Him wholeheartedly, and serve Him faithfully.

Who will be allowed to enter into the Millennial Kingdom?

The millennial kingdom is an exclusive reign, which will only include the tribulation saints (including Jews and Gentiles) and those who have part in the first resurrection (the church, Old Testament saints, and martyrs of the great tribulation) (Rev. 20:4-6).

Among the tribulation saints, there will be a great number who will not be killed, but will live through the Tribulation Period into the millennial kingdom. They will not possess glorified bodies like the believers who had been raptured prior to the Tribulation Period and the martyrs of the great tribulation who had been raised back to life with glorified bodies at the second coming of Christ. Since they don't possess glorified bodies, they will continue to live normal lives by entering into marriage relationships and having children during the millennial kingdom.

Even though all who entered the millennial kingdom will be saved forever, their children will have to decide for themselves whether they will have Christ as their Lord and Saviour. Not everyone will acknowledge Christ in their lives, but the Lord will allow them to live if they abide by the rules of the kingdom. Don't be mistaken, they will not possess eternal life, but such will be brought before the Great White Throne judgment at the end of the millennial kingdom to be judged.

The Purpose of the Millennial Kingdom

God does not do anything without a purpose. We may not fully understand now all of the divine purposes of the millennial kingdom, but we know a few that the Lord has graciously revealed to us in the Bible. These are sufficient for our finite minds to appreciate it.

1. **It will be the fulfillment of God's promise to Israel through David regarding his kingdom.** God promised David that his kingdom shall be established forever, fulfilling it through Christ who is a descendent of David. Thus He will occupy the throne of His father David fully as a Man. *"But my mercy shall not depart away from him, as I took it from Saul, whom I put away before thee. And thine house and thy kingdom shall be established for ever before thee: thy throne shall be established for ever"* (2 Sam. 7:15-16). The plan that God had decreed in the eternity passed regarding His Son's kingdom was promised to David. The fulfillment of this promise proves the faithfulness of God. No one can stand in the way of God's purposes, nor alter His purposes.

2. **It will also be to prove to the world that God is just and righteous in all His dealings with mankind, especially in relation to His judgments.** Humanity has questioned the justice of God in dealing with the evil acts committed by men throughout the centuries. Many of them are not convinced of God's position in these actions. But the millennial reign of Christ will serve the purpose of proving to the world that God is just and righteous in all His dealings with humanity. God finally will be vindicated by His righteousness. Today, many try to appease their guilt by putting the blame on Satan as the instigator of their evil deeds. But the millennial conditions will prove that man's heart is wicked even in the absence of Satan's deceptions. *"And when the thousand years are expired, Satan shall be loosed out of his prison, And shall go out to deceive*

the nations which are in the four quarters of the earth, Gog, and Magog, to gather them together to battle: the number of whom is as the sand of the sea" (Rev. 20:7-8).

3. **It will be the fulfillment of the promise Christ made during His earthly life to those who would believe in Him.** While the Lord Jesus was on this earth, He preached that the kingdom of God is at hand, and that those who would repent of their ways and turn to Him would be granted entrance to the kingdom of God. *"Jesus answered and said unto him, Verily, verily, I say unto thee, Except a man be born again, he cannot see the kingdom of God"* (John 3:3). The fulfillment of this promise will prove the veracity of His words. The Lord is not a leader who makes empty promises, but one who has the will and the ability to bring to fruition all that He promised. The world has seen so many leaders who make empty promises but the Lord Jesus is not one of them.

The Administration of the Millennial Kingdom

1. **Kingship of this kingdom**—The form of governance in this kingdom will neither be democratic nor autocratic, but theocratic. Christ will be the King of this kingdom. He will be the Supreme Ruler governing His kingdom according to His good will and pleasure. *"And they lived and reigned with Christ a thousand years"* (Rev. 20:4). Who are the "they" that lived and reigned with Christ? They are the ones who have enthroned Christ as their King in their hearts and lived accordingly. They shall be rewarded for their present service to the Lord by honouring them with the privilege of living and reigning with Christ. Will you be part of the "they" that lived and reigned with Christ? *"For the LORD is our judge, the LORD is our lawgiver, the Lord is our king; he will save us"* (Isa. 33:22).

2. **Administrative Center**—Jerusalem will be the capital of the world and also the administrative center of

the millennial kingdom. *"And it shall come to pass, that every one that is left of all the nations which came against Jerusalem shall even go up from year to year to worship the King, the Lord of hosts, and to keep the feast of tabernacles. And it shall be, that whoso will not come up of all the families of the earth unto Jerusalem to worship the King, the Lord of hosts, even upon them shall be no rain"* (Zech. 14:16-17). Jerusalem is now the epicenter of the conflict between the Palestinians and the Jews. Jerusalem is "one of the foundations of Israel's unity."[12] –Prime Minister Binyamin Netanyahu. But during the millennial kingdom, Jerusalem will rise to its full glory for the King of kings will be present there to receive the worship of His subjects.

3. **The Rule of Law**—Christ will rule the world with absolute righteousness. Now we live in a world where even in the most law abiding countries and form of governments, there is corruption, injustice, inequality, and unfair practices. As long as we live under the present conditions, we will continue to have these issues because we are imperfect and the world that we live in is fallen too.

> *And shall make him of quick understanding in the fear of the Lord: and he shall not judge after the sight of his eyes, neither reprove after the hearing of his ears: But with righteousness shall he judge the poor, and reprove with equity for the meek of the earth: and he shall smite the earth with the rod of his mouth, and with the breath of his lips shall he slay the wicked. And righteousness shall be the girdle of his loins, and faithfulness the girdle of his reins.*   Isaiah 11:3-5

The King is no longer a mere man, but God as well. This will affect how judgments are made and the rule of law

---

12   http://www.jpost.com/DiplomacyAndPolitics/Article.aspx?id=222682

is practiced. Decisions will not be made on hearsay, but upon truth. This would be the ideal government to be under for its King is righteous and faithful.

4. **Immediate Punishment**—Since this kingdom shall be ruled with absolute righteousness, there will be immediate repercussions for violations and disobedience. Such violators will be sentenced to death. *"Thou shalt break them with a rod of iron; thou shalt dash them in pieces like a potter's vessel"* (Ps. 2:9). Who are these violators? These are the children of the tribulation saints and the Gentile nations that favoured the Jews during the Tribulation Period. These children who grow up during the millennial kingdom will not get a free pass to eternal life by virtue of their parent's faith in Christ. They will have to believe in Christ for themselves just like their parents did while they lived through the Tribulation Period. The ones that will reject Christ and rebel against Him in their hearts will break the laws of the kingdom openly, and therefore, they will be sentenced to death. Such open violations will be significantly less than the present day crimes and violations of the law.

Conditions in the Millennial Kingdom

Even though the living conditions during the millennial kingdom will be not be perfect, it will surely be near perfect compared to the present living conditions. It will be a time of peace and harmony not only for the human race, but also for the animal kingdom, for creation will be restored. This will be a prelude to the eternal state for the saved. The following are some of the conditions that will prevail during the millennial kingdom:

1. **Life will continue as normal for Jews and Gentile nations who survived the Great Tribulation and are allowed to enter the millennial kingdom without glorified bodies.**

And they shall build houses, and inhabit them; and they shall plant vineyards, and eat the fruit of them. They shall not build, and another inhabit; they shall not plant, and another eat: for as the days of a tree are the days of my people, and mine elect shall long enjoy the work of their hands. They shall not labour in vain, nor bring forth for trouble; for they are the seed of the blessed of the Lord, and their offspring with them. Isaiah 65:21-23

People will go about doing their daily business, building homes to live in and work for their livelihood. But the difference is that they will be able to enjoy the fruit of their labor, for they shall live long enough to enjoy it. Today, life is so short and transient where one may not be able to enjoy a home that he built or enjoy retirement because he or she died unexpectedly. Today, we have so many unfulfilled desires and wishes, but during the millennial kingdom, people will live long enough to enjoy life.

2. **There will be close to perfect conditions in all areas of life.** There will be a sense of joy and satisfaction in the lives of people. There will be no reason to weep or cry. Can you image a society or culture of life where there will be no more weeping? Yet that will be the experience of those living during the millennial kingdom. *"But be ye glad and rejoice for ever in that which I create: for, behold, I create Jerusalem a rejoicing, and her people a joy. And I will rejoice in Jerusalem, and joy in my people: and the voice of weeping shall be no more heard in her, nor the voice of crying"* (Isa. 65:18-19). I believe this is what every human soul longs for, but the question is how do we achieve it? No matter what we try to do, the peace, joy, and satisfaction that is described here will never be achievable by any of our efforts. Rather, it is a result of

what Christ has done over 2,000 years ago on an old rugged cross.

What is it that Christ has done that has such lasting results? The Bible teaches that all the suffering and pain that we experience now is as a result of sin.

> *And unto Adam he said, Because thou hast hearkened unto the voice of thy wife, and hast eaten of the tree, of which I commanded thee, saying, Thou shalt not eat of it: cursed is the ground for thy sake; in sorrow shalt thou eat of it all the days of thy life; Thorns also and thistles shall it bring forth to thee; and thou shalt eat the herb of the field; In the sweat of thy face shalt thou eat bread, till thou return unto the ground; for out of it wast thou taken: for dust thou art, and unto dust shalt thou return.*
>
> Genesis 3:17-19

God brought the curse upon nature and man because of their disobedience. Hence, God took the initiative to put an end to this by sending His own Son – Jesus (who was sinless and holy) into this world to die in our place and pay the penalty for our sins. He was judged by God for our sins. Therefore, now, God can righteously bless us and undo the curse that was upon nature and mankind. Isn't God wonderful and His acts mighty and excellent? *"And the ransomed of the* LORD *shall return, and come to Zion with songs and everlasting joy upon their heads: they shall obtain joy and gladness, and sorrow and sighing shall flee away"* (Isa. 35:10).

3. **There will be perfect communion with Christ and His people.** *"And it shall come to pass, that before they call, I will answer; and while they are yet speaking, I will hear"* (Isa. 65:24). Even though presently we commune with God on a daily basis, we don't have perfect communion because of sin in our lives, and this inhibits God

from answering our prayers right away or granting what we might have asked for. But during the millennial kingdom, we will have perfect communion with God, live in sinless perfection, and know the perfect will of God. There will be no delay in God answering our request. In fact, while we are still speaking to God, He will hear and answer.

4. **There shall be a mighty outpouring of the Holy Spirit upon all flesh.** *"And it shall come to pass afterward, that I will pour out my spirit upon all flesh; and your sons and your daughters shall prophesy, your old men shall dream dreams, your young men shall see visions: And also upon the servants and upon the handmaids in those days will I pour out my spirit"* (Joel 2:28-29). What happened on the Day of Pentecost was a foretaste of what would happen during the millennial kingdom.

> *And when the day of Pentecost was fully come, they were all with one accord in one place. And suddenly there came a sound from heaven as of a rushing mighty wind, and it filled all the house where they were sitting. And there appeared unto them cloven tongues like as of fire, and it sat upon each of them. And they were all filled with the Holy Ghost, and began to speak with other tongues, as the Spirit gave them utterance.*
>
> Acts 2:1-4

There were mighty acts that were performed as a result of this outpouring of the Holy Spirit upon His disciples. A similar outpouring of the Holy Spirit will come upon all the people during the millennial kingdom, except it will be the perfect fulfillment of this prophecy by Joel. Imagine what life would be like when we will be perfectly indwelled and filled by the Holy Spirit, empowered and directed by the Holy Spirit.

5. **The Jewish temple worship will be reinstituted in Jerusalem.** It is not the reinstitution of the Old Testament sacrificial system, but the establishment of a new order of sacrifices where it is offered as memorial sacrifices instead of for the remission of sins (Ezek. 40-44). Now, in the church, we observe the Lord's Supper regularly not for the remission of sins, but as a memorial, celebrating the finished work of Christ over 2,000 years ago.

On the cross, Christ won victory over sin when He sacrificed His life as a payment for the penalty of our sins. To commemorate that great and glorious work of Christ to save us, we now observe the Lord's Supper. Moreover, the Lord commanded His disciples to observe it until He comes. Similarly, during the millennial kingdom, the sacrifices will be reinstituted not for the atonement of sin, but to celebrate and remember that mighty work of Christ. When we witness the animal sacrifices, it will put a new meaning to the sacrifice of Christ. This suggests to us that the work of Christ on the cross for our sins will never be forgotten by the saved. It is the sacrifice of Christ that will always give us access into God's presence, and therefore, it will always be fresh in our minds even after we have been in heaven for ages.

6. **Warfare will be a thing of the past and peace will prevail throughout the earth.** "...*they shall beat their swords into plowshares, and their spears into pruninghooks: nation shall not lift up sword against nation, neither shall they learn war any more*" (Isa. 2:4). Ever since the beginning of human history, this world has seen hundreds of battles fought, with a great deal of bloodshed and conflicts between rivalries. War has devastated many families and has taken the lives of millions. Today, the world is facing constant threats of wars, and nations are piling up on weapons of mass destruction and investing in new and highly sophisticated weapons.

But when the Lord Jesus Christ takes over the world as its sovereign King, wars and conflicts will cease to exist. Therefore, there will be no need for the development of weapons. The resources that were once used to develop weapons will be invested into productive and superior purposes that will benefit mankind. Obviously, if there are no weapons and wars, there will be no need to learn war strategy anymore. The world will be transformed into a peaceful place as the Lord originally intended in the creation of the world.

7. **Life expectancy will be greatly increased during the millennial kingdom.** *"There shall be no more thence an infant of days, nor an old man that hath not filled his days: for the child shall die an hundred years old; but the sinner being an hundred years old shall be accursed"* (Isa. 65:20). Today the infant mortality is 2.4% according to the World Health Organization.[13] But during the millennial kingdom, there will be no infant deaths, and instead a one hundred year old person is still considered a child. This is what God originally intended for the human race when He created them. But man disobeyed God and became subject to death—both physical and spiritual death. Life expectancy has been decreasing since then until now. During the millennial kingdom, God will supernaturally increase the life expectancy of those who have not believed in Christ (these are the children of the tribulation saints and the Gentile nations that favoured the Jews during the Tribulation Period). This is not applicable to any other group of people (Old Testament saints, New Testament saints, Tribulation saints) for they already possess glorified bodies and will never die. Those who possess glorified bodies (bodies that transformed from their present condition) will live forever.

---

13 http://www.who.int/gho/publications/world_health_statistics/EN_WHS2011_Full.pdf

8. **Sickness and deformity will be wiped out during the millennial kingdom.** *"And the inhabitant shall not say, I am sick: the people that dwell therein shall be forgiven their iniquity"* (Isa. 33:24). Today people are suffering from all kinds of sicknesses ranging from a minor cold to terminal illnesses like cancer and cardiovascular diseases. According to the World Health Organization, there are 12,420 diseases categorized in ICD-10.[14] Just in the United States there are over 11,958,000 people suffering from cancer.[15] The debilitating effort of illnesses have taken a toll on the human race regardless of the age of its victims. With the advancement of medical science and technology, there has been significant improvement in the treatment and eradication of certain diseases, but there are still diseases for which there are no cures. *"Then the eyes of the blind shall be opened, and the ears of the deaf shall be unstopped. Then shall the lame man leap as an hart, and the tongue of the dumb sing…"* (Isa. 35:5-6). According to the Human Genome Project, "there are more than 6,000 known single-gene disorders, which occur in about 1 out of every 200 births."[16] How devastating it is to see infants born with deformities or disabilities.

Why do we have sicknesses in the first place? Sickness is as a result of man's fall from his original state of sinless perfection. God has allowed sickness to come upon the human race because of their disobedience and rebellion against God. When we study the covenants of blessing that God had promised the Israelites, we will notice that it was conditional. If they obeyed God's commandments and followed His ways, God promised to take away from them all of their sickness. *"Wherefore it shall come to pass, if ye hearken to these*

---

14   http://www.who.int/classifications/help/icdfaq/en/index.html

15   http://www.cancer.org/Cancer/CancerBasics/cancer-prevalence

16   http://www.ornl.gov/sci/techresources/Human_Genome/medicine/assist.shtml

judgments, and keep, and do them, that the Lord thy God shall keep unto thee the covenant and the mercy which he sware unto thy fathers...And the Lord will take away from thee all sickness, and will put none of the evil diseases of Egypt, which thou knowest, upon thee; but will lay them upon all them that hate thee" (Deut. 7:12, 15).

Even today among believers, sickness can come about as a result of disobedience and unholy living. In relation to the observance of the Lord's Supper, the Apostle Paul implies that many among the Corinthian believers were weak and sick because of their sin and the unworthy manner in which they observed it. *"For he that eateth and drinketh unworthily, eateth and drinketh damnation to himself, not discerning the Lord's body. For this cause many are weak and sickly among you, and many sleep"* (1 Cor. 11:29-30). But one needs to be careful in drawing conclusions and judging when someone is sick. Let us be clear, as far as Christians are concerned, not all sickness is the result of sin.

Originally, when Adam and Eve sinned, sickness came as a byproduct of death. *"Wherefore, as by one man sin entered into the world, and death by sin; and so death passed upon all men, for that all have sinned"* (Rom. 5:12). When death invaded the human race, sickness was a means to accomplish it. People die because of some illness that has invaded their bodies or an accident that induced damage to their bodies or due to the gradual degradation of their bodies as they age. But what a relief from sickness for those of us who shall live during the millennial kingdom, when we shall possess glorified bodies!

9. **Death will be the exception and not the general rule during the millennial kingdom.** Now in this present age, death is the rule because God had decreed it. *"And as it is appointed unto men once to die, but after this the judgment"* (Heb. 9:27). During the millennial

kingdom the number of deaths will be significantly reduced because the vast majority of the people that will be living shall possess eternal life and glorified bodies. Death will come upon only those who reject Christ in their hearts and openly disobey and vehemently violate His orders and laws. These will be put to death.

10. **Creation will be restored during the millennial kingdom.**

> *For the earnest expectation of the creature waiteth for the manifestation of the sons of God. For the creature was made subject to vanity, not willingly, but by reason of him who hath subjected the same in hope Because the creature itself also shall be delivered from the bondage of corruption into the glorious liberty of the children of God. For we know that the whole creation groaneth and travaileth in pain together until now.*
>
> Romans 8:19-22

Nature will be restored to its original glory as God had created it in the beginning. Only Adam and Eve knew of the beauty and splendors of the original creation before its fall and ruin. *"And the Lord God planted a garden eastward in Eden; and there he put the man whom he had formed. And out of the ground made the Lord God to grow every tree that is pleasant to the sight, and good for food"* (Gen. 2:8-9a). What we presently see, as far as natural beauty, however spectacular it may be, is not what God created in the Garden of Eden. It is really a distorted view of the original creation.

When Adam and Eve disobeyed God's command they experienced a gradual decline of nature's beauty and its ability to yield its produce as it should. This was a direct consequence of God's curse upon the ground. This curse caused creation to groan and be subject to corruption. God said to Adam,

Because thou hast hearkened unto the voice of thy wife, and hast eaten of the tree, of which I commanded thee, saying, Thou shalt not eat of it: cursed is the ground for thy sake; in sorrow shalt thou eat of it all the days of thy life; Thorns also and thistles shall it bring forth to thee; and thou shalt eat the herb of the field; In the sweat of thy face shalt thou eat bread. Genesis 3:17-19

Now there are so many things that interfere with nature and its ability to bring forth its best and shine forth the glory of God. But during the millennial kingdom, the curse that now prevails upon nature will be withdrawn by God and creation will be restored to its original beauty and glory. Not only will it be restored, but there will no longer be corruption in the creation order. Imagine what a wonderful world it will be to live in!

11. **There shall be reconciliation of all things during the millennial kingdom.** *"For it pleased the Father that in him should all fulness dwell; And, having made peace through the blood of his cross"* (Col. 1:19-20). In this present world there are so many un-reconciled things, things that are out of place, things that are broken, things that are destroyed as a result of the fall and sin. It is true that the foundational work for the reconciliation of all things was accomplished over 2,000 years ago through the sacrificial death of Christ on the cross. But the full effect of His work will only be evident in the world during the millennial kingdom and beyond. Yes, surely we enjoy the manifold blessings of that mighty work of Christ, but not to its fullest, while we live in these vile bodies of ours and in this fallen, sin-stricken world. The magnitude and efficacy of the blood of Christ will only be fully understood when we live in our glorified bodies and in a restored world. Then we will marvel at the magnificent work

of Christ, in its redeeming power, and its significance in the grand plan of God.

12. **Wild animals will be tamed and friendly in the millennial kingdom.** *"And the sucking child shall play on the hole of the asp, and the weaned child shall put his hand on the cockatrice' den. They shall not hurt nor destroy in all my holy mountain"* (Isa. 11:8-9). *"The wolf and the lamb shall feed together, and the lion shall eat straw like the bullock: and dust shall be the serpant's meat. They shall not hurt nor destroy in all my holy mountain, saith the Lord"* (Isa. 65:25). The vicious nature of wild animals came about as a result of the fall. If you read the creation account in Genesis, there you will notice that Adam lived with the animals and was in charge and in absolute control over them. *"And out of the ground the Lord God formed every beast of the field, and every fowl of the air; and brought them unto Adam to see what he would call them: and whatsoever Adam called every living creature, that was the name thereof. And Adam gave names to all cattle, and to the fowl of the air, and to every beast of the field"* (Gen. 2:19-20a). The devastating effect of man's sin not only ruined his life, but put a great toll on the animal kingdom as well. Man is not in harmony with the animal kingdom, but a rivalry exists that creates a sense of fear within them. But all of that will be restored during the millennial kingdom and man will be in perfect harmony with the animal kingdom. Notice, even children will play with cobras and vipers and they shall not hurt them. This will be true of all wild animals. They will be subject to mankind's control.

13. **The animal kingdom will co-exist in peace and harmony during the millennial kingdom.** *"The wolf also shall dwell with the lamb, and the leopard shall lie down with the kid; and the calf and the young lion and the fatling together; and a little child shall lead them. And the cow and*

the bear shall feed; their young ones shall lie down together" (Isa. 11:6-7). *"The wolf and the lamb shall feed together"* (Isa. 65:25a). Not only is there no peace and harmony between humans and the animal kingdom, but there is no harmony even within the animal kingdom. The reason for such chaos and viciousness within the animal kingdom currently is because of the fallen world in which we live. In today's world, the lamb and the goat are prey to the wolf, but in the millennial kingdom, the wolf and the lamb shall live together in peace. Notice, little children shall lead them. What a peaceful and harmonious world that would be!

14. **All animals will be herbivorous in the millennial kingdom.** *"…the lion shall eat straw like the bullock: and dust shall be the serpent's meat"* (Isa. 65:25).

DESCENDING OF THE HOLY CITY NEW JERUSALEM

The Inhabitants of New Jerusalem

The bride of Christ or the Lamb's wife and possibly the Old Testament saints shall be its inhabitants.

> *And there came unto me one of the seven angels which had the seven vials full of the seven last plagues, and talked with me, saying, Come hither, I will shew thee the bride, the Lamb's wife… And had a wall great and high, and had twelve gates, and at the gates twelve angels, and names written thereon, which are the names of the twelve tribes of the children of Israel: On the east three gates; on the north three gates; on the south three gates; and on the west three gates. And the wall of the city had twelve foundations, and in them the names of the twelve apostles of the Lamb.*
>
> Revelation 21:9, 12-14

The New Jerusalem will be the dwelling place of the bride of Christ, the church, but the fact that it has the names of the twelve tribes of the children of Israel on its gates suggests that it will be the dwelling place of the Old Testament saints as well. That is not going to diminish its glory or take away from the bride of Christ any ability to fully enjoy it, rather it will surely enrich it.

The Location of New Jerusalem

It will be in the heaven (atmospheric), above the city of Jerusalem. *"And he carried me away in the spirit to a great and high mountain, and shewed me that great city, the holy Jerusalem, descending out of heaven from God"* (Rev. 21:10). Notice, it will descend out of heaven but not necessarily land on earth. It is suspended in the atmosphere above the earth providing access to earth on which are the rest of the people who don't possess glorified bodies. To transport oneself from the New Jerusalem to the earth will not be difficult for one who possesses a glorified body.

The Architect of New Jerusalem

God Himself will be the Architect of it. *"And he carried me away in the spirit to a great and high mountain, and shewed me that great city, the holy Jerusalem, descending out of heaven from God"* (Rev. 21:10). The New Jerusalem is the exclusive work of God and we can only imagine how awesome and glorious it will be. Not man nor any other being will have any part in the design and building of the New Jerusalem for it is from God.

The Structure of New Jerusalem

It had a great and high wall with twelve gates. The wall of the city was 200 feet high and had twelve foundations made out of precious stones. The street of the city was pure gold, like transparent glass. The city measured 1,400 miles in length, breadth, and height and looks like a square. What is this enormous structure?

And he carried me away in the spirit to a great and high mountain, and shewed me that great city, the holy Jerusalem, descending out of heaven from God, Having the glory of God: and her light was like unto a stone most precious, even like a jasper stone, clear as crystal; And had a wall great and high, and had twelve gates, and at the gates twelve angels, and names written thereon, which are the names of the twelve tribes of the children of Israel: On the east three gates; on the north three gates; on the south three gates; and on the west three gates. And the wall of the city had twelve foundations, and in them the names of the twelve apostles of the Lamb. And he that talked with me had a golden reed to measure the city, and the gates thereof, and the wall thereof. And the city lieth foursquare, and the length is as large as the breadth: and he measured the city with the reed, twelve thousand furlongs. The length and the breadth and the height of it are equal. And he measured the wall thereof, an hundred and forty and four cubits, according to the measure of a man, that is, of the angel. And the building of the wall of it was of jasper: and the city was pure gold, like unto clear glass. And the foundations of the wall of the city were garnished with all manner of precious stones. The first foundation was jasper; the second, sapphire; the third, a chalcedony; the fourth, an emerald; The fifth, sardonyx; the sixth, sardius; the seventh, chrysolyte; the eighth, beryl; the ninth, a topaz; the tenth, a chrysoprasus; the eleventh, a jacinth; the twelfth, an amethyst. And the twelve gates were twelve pearls: every several gate was of one pearl: and the street of the city was pure gold, as it were transparent glass. Revelation 21:10-21

It will be a magnificent city unlike any city that we have ever seen in this world. It will be made out of precious stones of which twelve will be laid as foundations. The walls will be made of jasper and the city and its streets will be of pure gold transparent as clear glass. It will be breathtaking and grand.

And who is it for? It's for unworthy people like us, who were sinners and rebels. But God in His infinite love and grace chose to love us and save us by sending His own Son—Jesus into this wicked world to die on our behalf for our sins. Isn't that awesome? You can have this glorious prospect of eternity and blessedness of dwelling in the New Jerusalem, if you would now come to God in repentance and by faith accept Christ as your personal Saviour and Lord. That is all God is asking you to do. *"That if thou shalt confess with thy mouth the Lord Jesus, and shalt believe in thine heart that God hath raised him from the dead, thou shalt be saved. For with the heart man believeth unto righteousness; and with the mouth confession is made unto salvation. For the scripture saith, Whosoever believeth on him shall not be ashamed"* (Rom. 10:9-11). Don't delay this most important decision in your life; make it right now. God will honour your decision and accept you as you are. Otherwise, you will miss the opportunity to enjoy eternity with God and receive His wonderful blessings that are reserved for His children.

THE FINAL REVOLT OF SATAN AND THE NATIONS

Even though there will be peace and harmony throughout the millennial kingdom, after the duration of the millennial kingdom is complete, there will be a final revolt of Satan and the nations against Christ. God will allow Satan to revolt against Him to prove the wickedness of man's heart even after experiencing firsthand the glorious reign of Christ in peace, righteousness, justice, and splendor. It will be the ultimate proof that man rejects God and His offer of salvation not because God rejected them, but because man had rejected God in his heart. This will prove that God is righteous, just, and fair in all His dealings with mankind.

The Duration of the Final Revolt of Satan

It is not specified, but it seems to be rapid. This will not be an elaborate battle like the campaign during the Great Tribulation, but a quick response by the Lord Jesus that will settle the unrest and revolt.

When will the Final Revolt take place?

This revolt will only occur after the 1,000 years reign of Christ and the release of Satan from his prison by Christ. *"And when the thousand years are expired, Satan shall be loosed out of his prison, And shall go out to deceive the nations which are in the four quarters of the earth, Gog and Magog, to gather them together to battle: the number of whom is as the sand of the sea"* (Rev. 20:7-8). One thing to realize is that Satan is powerful, but he is still subject to Christ and cannot do anything without the permission of Christ. But that is not what Satan wants us to believe and perceive of him.

Satan will not deceive the nations or influence them in any way during the millennial kingdom, but once Satan is released from his captivity, he will be allowed to do what he has been doing since his fall, and that is to deceive people into joining him against God. The deception is not to reject Christ at that point, but to rally and form an alliance among those who have already rejected Christ inwardly during the millennial kingdom. Notice the subtle way Satan goes about forming an alliance. The only people who will fall into this alliance will be the children (born during the millennial kingdom) of those who survived the Great Tribulation and entered into the millennial kingdom. Since they have rejected Christ, in spite of clear and explicit evidences of Christ's Lordship and instructions to obey and follow Christ, they will now openly reject Christ along with Satan. There is no middle ground, rejection of Christ means acceptance of Satan. It is quite possible to think of yourself as a good person, and it may be true comparatively, but if you haven't accepted Christ as your Saviour and Lord, then your alliance is truly with Satan.

The number of those who will form alliance with Satan is described as "the sand of the sea". Obviously, it will not be a small group, but a large number, which again demonstrates man's hatred of God and the wickedness of his heart. *"The heart is deceitful above all things, and desperately wicked: who can know it?"* (Jer. 17:9). Since man's heart is deceitful, he will reject Christ even after witnessing firsthand His sovereignty, love, grace, justice, and omnipotence. What a depressing state of affairs? That is why it is so important to respond to God's call to repentance right away and do not delay. *"To day if ye will hear his voice, harden not your hearts, as in the provocation"* (Heb. 3:15).

How will Satan orchestrate this revolt against Christ?

Once Satan is released from his prison, he will swiftly go throughout the earth to deceive the nations into a final revolt against Christ and His people because he knows his time is limited and his plans are going to be shattered forever. His tool he will use in his final revolt is deception and that is what he has been using since the creation of mankind. Since he can only deceive those who have not believed in Christ, the task is easy and quick. This will be his final and last attempt in disturbing and derailing God's plans and purposes. He does this not because he thinks he can, but because he has no other option and as a final demonstration of his hatred of God. Satan is obviously not involved in building up people's lives but in destroying them. If you think you're better off on Satan's side, please think twice. Your life is heading to destruction while you are enjoying pleasures during your few years on earth.

How will Christ defeat Satan and his followers?

The Lord doesn't go into an elaborate display of power like He did during the Tribulation Period; instead He devours the nations by fire that comes down from God out of heaven. Then, Satan is cast into the lake of fire for whom it was created. *"and fire came down from God out of heaven, and devoured them. And the devil that deceived them was cast into the lake of fire and brimstone"* (Rev. 20:9-10a). This marks the end of Satan's revolt against God once and for all. He will no longer be able to stand in the path of God's plans and purposes. Satan - the enemy of God, who brought about the fall of mankind and the devastation of pain and suffering that followed it, will be forever cast into the lake of fire, no more able to deceive people, torment God's people, and dishonour the name of God. What a glorious victory for the Lord God Almighty! This great triumph was brought about by the redemptive work of Christ on the cross over 2,000 years ago, on a mount called Calvary, by a Man who was mocked, ridiculed, disowned by the religious authorities, and rejected by His own people. The Man who is truly God has finally put an end to Satan and his cohorts.

What is the eternal destiny of Satan?

Satan will be forever cast into the lake of fire where he will suffer the eternal wrath of God for all the destruction that he has brought upon God's creation. It is probable that the fallen angels (demons) could also be cast into the lake of fire along with Satan at this time. Satan's followers will follow him to their eternal destiny as well. *"For if God spared not the angels that sinned, but cast them down to hell, and delivered them into chains of darkness, to be reserved unto judgment"* (2 Pet. 2:4). *"And the angels which kept not their first estate, but left their own habitation, he hath reserved in everlasting chains under darkness unto the judgment of the great day"* (Jude 6). Among the fallen angels there are some who are reserved presently in everlasting chains in hell, thus limiting their ability to act on behalf of Satan, and there are some who are free to roam under the command of their leader, Satan.

Another reason why the fallen angels might be judged and cast into the lake of fire after the duration of the millennial kingdom (even though they might be incarcerated along with Satan during the 1000 years of Christ's reign) is that it is said to occur on "the judgment of the great day", which is a reference to the time period of the Great White Throne judgment. *"Know ye not that we shall judge angels?"* (1 Cor. 6:3). The believers, who are glorified, along with Christ, will be part of judging fallen angels as well as judging the world. Who are we to judge the fallen angels and the world? We were once sinners and rebels as they are, equally condemned and worthy of eternal hellfire, but by God's grace we have been translated from the kingdom of darkness into the kingdom of light. How devoted and consecrated our lives ought to be when we think of God's grace and love towards us!

THE GREAT WHITE THRONE JUDGMENT

The Great White Throne judgment is the final judgment of God as far as the revealed Word of God is concerned. It marks the end of God's judgment associated with evil in any form. If you appear before the Great White Throne judgment, there is no recourse; no offer of God's grace any longer, no more pardon. What awaits unbelievers is the continual wrath of God in the eternal lake of fire.

The Duration of the Great White Throne Judgment
It is not specified.

When will it take place?
It will take place immediately following the millennial rule of Christ and prior to the destruction of the heavens and earth with fire. If the rapture of the church were to occur today, it would take place 1007 years from now. But don't be fooled into thinking that since this event is so far into the future that somehow it would be delayed or sidetracked, maybe even cancelled, or destroyed by some catastrophic event, or that even God might change His mind. This judgment was decreed by God in eternity past and is recorded in the revealed Word of God. It is certain that this judgment will occur as God's Word declares. *"And as it is appointed unto men once to die, but after this the judgment"* (Heb. 9:27). Neither will time ease the significance nor the severity of this judgment, for God is not subject to time. God is ever present.

Where will it take place?

It seems like its setting is neither on earth nor in heaven, but some realm beyond these. *"And I saw a great white throne, and him that sat on it, from whose face the earth and the heaven fled away; and there was found no place for them"* (Rev. 20:11). Whatever the setting of this judgment will be it shall be beyond our wildest imagination. It is not a matter of where it will take place, but making sure you escape this coming judgment. If you're not certain about your eternal destiny, you should be concerned with how you can be freed from this coming judgment. Wherever it might take place, if you're not saved, you will have to appear there.

Who will be the Judge?

The Lord Jesus Christ will be the Judge who proclaims the verdict. *"And I saw a great white throne, and him that sat on it, from whose face the earth and the heaven fled away"* (Rev. 20:11). At the Great White Throne judgment, the Lord Jesus will be fulfilling His role as the righteous Judge, ensuring that the justice of God is revealed in the judgment of men and women from all ages, who have rejected God in spite of their knowledge of His existence and refusing to believe and please Him throughout their lives.

The Bible is very clear that no one who appears at this judgment will have a valid reason for not believing the living God and entering into a relationship with His Son—Jesus Christ.

For the invisible things of him from the creation of the world are clearly seen, being understood by the things that are made, even his eternal power and Godhead; so that they are without excuse: Because that, when they knew God, they glorified him not as God, neither were thankful; but became vain in their imaginations, and their foolish heart was darkened. Professing themselves to be wise, they became fools, And changed the glory of the uncorruptible God into an image made like to corruptible man, and to

*birds, and fourfooted beasts, and creeping things.
Wherefore God also gave them up to uncleanness
through the lusts of their own hearts, to dishonour
their own bodies between themselves: Who changed
the truth of God into a lie, and worshipped and
served the creature more than the Creator, who is
blessed for ever. Amen.*   Romans 1:20-25

The fact is that everyone has within them a moral com-
pass—the conscience that is given by God, that will attest to the
reality of God's existence. There is no doubt, that deep within
our hearts we know that there is a higher Being who is in absolute control of everything. In spite of this knowledge, some
choose to ignore it or, in many cases, reject it and live according
to their evil passions and desires. This leads many to fashion a
god to their liking, leading to the formation of idols, manmade
religions and a philosophical approach to God.

Everyone whose name is not found written in the Book of
Life will be summoned to appear before the Judge of all—the
Lord Jesus Christ. If you die today, will you have to appear
before the Great White Throne judgment? You can have the
absolute assurance that you will not have to appear for this
judgment based on the fact that you decided to repent of your
sins and accept Christ as your Saviour and Lord by faith. Don't
take any chances, make it certain right now. If you make that
decision sincerely, then you will not appear before the Great
White Throne judgment, but will be part of the glorious blessings of God in heaven.

Who will be judged?

All of the dead unsaved people of all times will be resurrected to appear before the Judge—the Lord Jesus Christ.
*"And I saw the dead, small and great, stand before God; and the
books were opened...And the sea gave up the dead which were in it;
and death and hell delivered up the dead which were in them"* (Rev.
20:12-13). No matter who you are, if your name is not found
in the Book of Life you will be judged to eternal punishment.

Notice that whether you are "small or great" while alive makes no difference to the kind of judgment you will receive from the righteous and holy God. Kings will stand next to common men, the rich will stand next to the poor, the intellectual will stand next to the foolish, the religious will stand next to the atheist, and such will be the contrast of those who stand before the Great White Throne Judgment! *"For there is no respect of persons with God"* (Rom. 2:11).

What will be the basis for the judgment?

This judgment will not be to determine whether or not one will inherit eternal life or eternal punishment, rather it will be to determine the degree of punishment in hell for those who are already condemned. *"And that servant, which knew his lord's will, and prepared not himself, neither did according to his will, shall be beaten with many stripes. But he that knew not, and did commit things worthy of stripes, shall be beaten with few stripes. For unto whomsoever much is given, of him shall be much required: and to whom men have committed much, of him they will ask the more"* (Luke 12:47-48).

Anyone who hasn't believed in the Lord Jesus is condemned already. *"He that believeth on him is not condemned: but he that believeth not is condemned already, because he hath not believed in the name of the only begotten Son of God"* (John 3:18). The Great White Throne judgment will not be the place where one will be judged as to their eternal destination—heaven or hell, but only the condemned will appear there. They are condemned not because God did not like them, but because they did not believe in Christ as their personal Saviour and Lord. They did not accept Christ as the only way to God, the only One who can forgive their sins, and the only One who can save them from eternal condemnation.

The books were opened in which are the deeds of every person to determine the degree of punishment. The Book of Life was opened to prove to the individual that he or she is not saved because his or her name is not in it. This is sufficient evidence before the God of justice to condemn a person to eternal punishment. *"The books were opened: and another book was opened, which is the book of life: and the dead were judged out of those things which were written in the books...and they were judged every man according to their works...And whosoever was not found written in the book of life was cast into the lake of fire"* (Rev. 20:12-13, 15). Another book was opened, which contained the deeds of everyone. It will be based on this book that one will be judged as to the degree of his or her punishment. Can you imagine that God records every deed of ours in a book that is kept in heaven? It is not too hard for the Lord to record your life, for He is the Almighty God. If you think that your present actions have no consequences, you're wrong. As a matter of fact, they have eternal consequences, which is even more serious and deserves our utmost attention. It is going to determine where you will spend your eternity. You can rest assured that God is not going to make a mistake when it comes to your judgment because He is going to judge you according to your works. In other words, what did you do with what you knew of God? And He is not going to judge on the curve; everyone will receive the precise punishment that is due based on their deeds.

The fact that God revealed His standards of judgment in advance in the Bible, suggests that He is a loving God who desires that they might come to Christ by faith for their salvation and deliverance from eternal hell and wants people to conduct their lives in such a way that brings glory to God. Anyone who appears at the Great White Throne judgment will be there because of their willful rejection of God and His offer of salvation through Christ. There should be no doubt in the minds of people as to how God is going to judge them.

What will be the outcome of the judgment?

All those who appear before the Great White Throne Judgment will be cast into the lake of fire forever. The first death is the separation of the body from the spirit, which results in physical death, whereas the lake of fire is the second death, which is eternal separation from God. *"And death and hell were cast into the lake of fire. This is the second death. And whosoever was not found written in the book of life was cast into the lake of fire"* (Rev. 20:14-15). It will be a place of unending conscious suffering and pain like man has never experienced or ever conceived before. The severity of the punishment will not decrease as time passes because they will be under the constant wrath of God. There will be no change to the amount of pain and suffering. There will be heightened levels of desires and passions, but no way to fulfill it. For example, one will thirst for a drop of water in hell, but there will be no way to get a drop of water to quench thirst; one will regret what they have done with their lives while alive on the earth and the missed opportunities to trust in Christ, but there will be no way to change the outcome of the situation nor will there be any option to be freed. Can you imagine the mental agony of living such a life forever?

Is this really what you want for the rest of eternity? I hope you will not simply read over this without making a meaningful decision. No sin, no friendship, no activity, no addiction, nor any form of worldly pleasure is worth going to hell for. Your life is much more precious than anything you can ever imagine. That is why God sent His own beloved Son Jesus into this fallen world to be born supernaturally as an infant, live a perfect life as a man, and finally die a cursed death on the cross as the punishment for our sins, and be resurrected to life accomplishing the greatest victory that any religion, philosophy, or leader could ever have achieved. He now offers eternal life to all who would believe in Him and what He did. This is the simple message of the Bible that can change your life now and your eternal destiny.

PRESENT DAY IMPLICATIONS

1. Your responsibility in the millennial kingdom is dependent on your present faithfulness to the talents and spiritual gifts bestowed upon you.

2. If you suffer for Christ now, you will reign with Him in the kingdom.

3. The heart of man is desperately wicked, therefore, we should guard our hearts from evil by depending on the Holy Spirit.

4. Have you accepted Jesus Christ as your personal Saviour and Lord?

5. Are you sharing the gospel of Jesus Christ with the lost?

DECISIONS

Write down the decisions that you made in light of this chapter.

_____

_____

_____

_____

_____

_____

FIVE

THE ETERNAL STATE

Once the millennial reign of Christ comes to an end, the present earth and heaven will be purged by fire to create the new heaven and new earth. This paves the path to the eternal state, where God dwells with men forever. This will be the climax of God's dealing with man as far as in the revealed Scriptures.

MAJOR EVENTS INCLUDED IN THIS NEW DISPENSATION—FOREVER

1. Dissolving of the present earth and heaven by fire (Matt. 25:31-46)

2. Creation of the new heaven and new earth (Rev. 21:1, 2 Pet. 3:7, 10, 12)

3. Transfer of the kingdom of God (1 Cor. 15:24-28)

4. Life in the Eternal City – The New Jerusalem (Rev. 21:9-27)

DISSOLVING OF THE PRESENT EARTH AND HEAVEN BY FIRE

When will the present earth and heaven be dissolved?

The key to understanding the timeline is to note that the last event of the "day of the Lord" (spans from the rapture of the church through the Great White Throne judgment) is the dissolving of the old earth and the old heavens prior to ushering in the "day of God" (spans from the creation of the new heaven and new earth through eternity). This won't happen until the day of judgment and perdition of ungodly men, that is, the Great White Throne Judgment has occurred. *"But the heavens and the earth, which are now, by the same word are kept in store, reserved unto fire against the day of judgment and perdition of ungodly men…But the day of the Lord will come as a thief in the night; in the which the heavens shall pass away with a great noise, and the elements shall melt with fervent heat, the earth also and the works that are therein shall be burned up…Looking for and hasting unto the coming of the day of God, wherein the heavens being on fire shall be dissolved, and the elements shall melt with fervent heat?"* (2 Pet. 3:7, 10, 12).

According to God's Word, the present earth and the heavens (the atmospheric heaven) are reserved to be destroyed by fire like the floods that destroyed the world during the time of Noah. *"Heaven and earth shall pass away, but my words shall not pass away"* (Matt. 24:35). Just like the floods destroyed the world as God warned, the present world will be destroyed by fire. God has given us enough warning just as He did to the people that lived prior to the flood. This suggests that this world is not permanent and we should not store up or invest in this fallen world system, rather in heaven, which is eternal. *"Lay not up for yourselves treasures upon earth, where moth and rust doth corrupt, and where thieves break through and steal: But lay up for yourselves treasures in heaven, where neither moth nor rust doth corrupt, and where thieves do not break through nor steal: For where your treasure is, there will your heart be also"* (Matt. 6:19-21). If we invest our time, resources, and money in this world, it will be a waste since it will all be destroyed one day. But if we invest in heaven, it will yield great returns that will have eternal value.

The present earth and the heavens will be purged to produce a new earth and a new heaven. *"And I saw a new heaven and a new earth: for the first heaven and the first earth were passed away"* (Rev. 21:1).

Why should the earth and heaven be dissolved?

The dissolution of the present earth and heaven by fire is to purge out all traces of sin, the curse placed by God on earth when Adam sinned, and the last vestige of the fallen world. *"And, Thou, Lord, in the beginning hast laid the foundation of the earth; and the heavens are the works of thine hands: They shall perish; but thou remainest; and they all shall wax old as doth a garment; And as a vesture shalt thou fold them up, and they shall be changed"* (Heb. 1:10-12a). The present world is corrupted and will become even older and corrupt. This old world will not fit with the overall change that God will bring about, and so, it will be replaced with a new earth and a new heaven. But it is reasonable to believe that the new earth and the new heaven will be similar to the present one but with untold beauty and without degradation and traces of the fall that resulted from sin.

Moreover, the redeeming work of Christ has in it the power to restore everything that has been affected by sin and the fall to a new, perfect state of being. If the Lord doesn't restore this fallen world, then there would be a deficiency in Christ's work on the cross. The efficacy of the work of Christ is of infinite value. There is nothing that cannot be reconciled or restored from the fall.

CREATION OF THE NEW HEAVEN AND NEW EARTH

When will the new heaven and new earth be created?

It will occur probably after the purging of the present earth and heaven and as a result of it. *"And I saw a new heaven and a new earth: for the first heaven and the first earth were passed away; and there was no more sea"* (Rev. 21:1). The creation of the new heaven and new earth may have similar qualities to the original creation except it will be far superior. Creation will not only be restored, but it will also be preserved for eternity in all of its splendor.

We now live in a world that is practicing unrighteousness, but in the new earth, righteousness shall dwell. *"Nevertheless we, according to his promise, look for new heavens and a new earth, wherein dwelleth righteousness"* (2 Pet. 3:13). There will be no more traces of evil or unrighteousness, but what remains will be pure, holy, and righteous. Our present way of life – the pain and suffering will be a thing of the past once we possess glorified bodies and dwell in the new earth. *"For, behold, I create new heavens and a new earth: and the former shall not be remembered, nor come into mind"* (Isa. 65:17). What is referred to here as the former is limited to the way of life, and in that sense, we will not continue in it. We will still have the ability to comprehend the way that we lived on this earth. This will certainly enrich our comprehension of life in the new earth.

Why does God create the new heaven and new earth?

The new heaven is not in reference to the third heaven, for that is the eternal dwelling place of God, but here it is the atmospheric heaven that is under consideration. The new heaven and new earth will be needed to support life to its fullest under the new order of things. Since our bodies are going to be made perfect, a perfect environment will be ideal for our habitation. Another interesting thing to notice about the new earth is that there will be no more sea. Water as we know is essential for the present life, but in that eternal state water is non-essential. The removal of the sea could be to inhabit the vast population of saved people. Presently, a large population of saved people are in heaven and only a small population remains on the earth. And so, when all believers inhabit the earth, there needs to be space for all to live. It will not be crowded for sure; rather it will be magnificent and glorious. The new earth will be the eternal dwelling place of Israel and the nations, coexisting in perfect harmony and peace.

TRANSFER OF THE KINGDOM OF GOD

The kingdom over which Christ reigned as King for a thousand years will be handed over to God the Father after He had subdued all of His enemies and completely erased every trace of sin that Satan brought upon this world. All of Satan's plans will be nullified. Once everything has been reconciled to God and the old order of creation has been replaced with the new order of creation, Christ will have perfectly completed His Father's assignment. This will probably be the last event of the day of the Lord or perhaps, the first event of the day of God. Once the kingdom is handed over, Christ will subject Himself to the Father as the eternal Son of God, so that God (the Father, the Son, and the Holy Spirit) may be all in all. The Godhead will exist as it did in eternity past before creation.

> *Then cometh the end, when he shall have delivered up the kingdom to God, even the Father; when he shall have put down all rule and all authority and power. For he must reign, till he hath put all enemies under his feet. The last enemy that shall be destroyed is death. For he hath put all things under his feet. But when he saith all things are put under him, it is manifest that he is excepted, which did put all things under him. And when all things shall be subdued unto him, then shall the Son also himself be subject unto him that put all things under him, that God may be all in all.* 1 Corinthians 15:24-28

What a moment it will be in all of eternity, when God rests from all His labors and enters into rest along with His people, who will acknowledge God in perfection. It will be the climax of Christ's work, when everything is perfectly restored as God planned. There will be no more opposing forces or evil prevailing that will diminish God's glory, but from then on forever, God will be all in all. And the wonderful thing is that you can be part of that glorious moment when it takes place.

LIFE IN THE ETERNAL CITY— THE NEW JERUSALEM

Life will be so wonderful and exciting in the eternal city that no one will ever wish for anything different. Life in this city will be God-centered, which itself will make the whole experience something worth longing for. Our present life is filled with sorrow, pain, failures, struggles, and dangers, but life in the eternal city will be perfect beyond our wildest dreams. It will not be a match for any experience enjoyed anywhere in this world. Just a thought of life in the eternal city should evoke a sense of curiosity, creating a desire to investigate how one becomes eligible for it. If you're interested in possessing this eternal life, you only need to receive eternal life as a free gift through receiving Jesus Christ as your Lord and Saviour!

Perfect Environment

There will be no need for the sun or the moon to shine because the Lamb Himself is the light of that city. The glory that is radiated from God will light the new earth too. Now we experience God's light spiritually, but in that city we shall live directly under the radiance of God's light. *"And the city had no need of the sun, neither of the moon, to shine in it: for the glory of God did lighten it, and the Lamb is the light thereof. And the nations of them which are saved shall walk in the light of it: and the kings of the earth do bring their glory and honour into it. And the gates of it shall not be shut at all by day: for there shall be no night there"* (Rev. 21:23-25).

Perfect City

The New Jerusalem—that great city will be spectacular, breathtaking, and eternal. Human words are inadequate to describe its true beauty. *"And he carried me away in the spirit to a great and high mountain, and shewed me that great city, the holy Jerusalem, descending out of heaven from God, Having the glory of God"* (Rev. 21:10-11).

Perfect Communion

There shall be perfect communion between God and man, where God dwells with men. *"And I heard a great voice out of heaven saying, Behold, the tabernacle of God is with men, and he will dwell with them, and they shall be his people, and God himself shall be with them, and be their God"* (Rev. 21:3). It was God's original desire and plan to dwell among man, which He initiated with the establishment of the Old Testament Tabernacle. *"I will dwell among the children of Israel, and will be their God"* (Ex. 29:45). With the incarnation of Christ, this desire was introduced and put into motion. *"Behold, a virgin shall be with child, and shall bring forth a son, and they shall call his name Emmanuel, which being interpreted is, God with us"* (Matt. 1:23). Through the sacrifice of Christ this communion was extended to sinful people upon their faith in Christ. *"God is faithful, by whom ye were called unto the fellowship of his Son Jesus Christ our Lord"* (1 Cor. 1:9).

Can you imagine what it would be like to live with God face to face without any barriers? It is true that as believers we experience God's presence daily in our lives, but what we are going to experience in the eternal city is totally unparalleled. Notice the emphasis that *"God himself shall be with them"* so as to dismiss any thoughts that God would visit occasionally with His people. He will be permanently dwelling with His people, never to be separated for any reason.

Perfect Community

Life will be enjoyed in all of its perfection without any death, sorrow, pain, and tears. *"And God shall wipe away all tears from their eyes; and there shall be no more death, neither sorrow, nor crying, neither shall there be any more pain: for the former things are passed away"* (Rev. 21:4). God's people will dwell together forever and won't have to deal with life's challenges and struggles.

Perfect Access

The gates of that city will not be shut for there is no night there. *"And the gates of it shall not be shut at all by day: for there shall be no night there"* (Rev. 21:25). We now enjoy unlimited access to the throne of grace to find help in time of need, but in the eternal city, there will be perfect access in the sense that we will have no barriers in maintaining a constant access to God.

Perfect Holiness

There will be nothing that will ever defile that city, for everything that defiles has been removed and those that remain are perfect. *"And there shall in no wise enter into it any thing that defileth, neither whatsoever worketh abomination, or maketh a lie: but they which are written in the Lamb's book of life"* (Rev. 21:27). What remains from hereafter will be sinless perfection because only those whose names are written in the Lamb's Book of Life will be present in glorified bodies.

Perfect Life

There will be perfect life (the life of God), which flows constantly and infinitely from the throne of God. *"And he shewed me a pure river of water of life, clear as crystal, proceeding out of the throne of God and of the Lamb"* (Rev. 22:1). Our life will be nourished and supported by the very life of God.

Perfect Health

There will be the perfect enjoyment of health through the twelve fruits that the tree of life yields. *"In the midst of the street of it, and on either side of the river, was there the tree of life, which bare twelve manner of fruits, and yielded her fruit every month: and the leaves of the tree were for the healing of the nations"* (Rev. 22:2). In the eternal city there will be no more concerns about getting sick or taking medication to support life. Not only is our health a top concern but the cost of healthcare as well.[17] "In fact, in 2009, the average annual cost of health care was $7,960 per person." If the cost keeps going up, the majority of the people will not be able to afford basic healthcare services.

Imagine one morning waking up with perfect health and no more health related issues to be worried about. That is exactly what we will experience in our glorified bodies. Body aches, headaches, cancers, and AIDS will be a think of the past, even something as simple as common cold will not

---

17   http://www.pbs.org/newshour/rundown/2011/11/why-does-healthcare-cost-so-much.html

bother us anymore, for all sickness will be completely eradicated. These are not man-made fictional stories, but they are what the eternal God has promised for His people as documented in the Word of God. Knowing these things should transform our lives, to view life itself from God's perspective. Then these future events will be a reality in the lives of His people because God who cannot lie has promised it.

Perfect Service

There shall be perfect service to God with the absence of the curse, rebellion, and deception. *"And there shall be no more curse: but the throne of God and of the Lamb shall be in it; and his servants shall serve him"* (Rev. 22:3). Even though we will be enjoying perfect rest from all our present labor and toils, we will still continue to serve God in eternity. We will then have the ability to serve perfectly without any impure motives.

Perfect Identification

We shall forever be identified with the Lord by bearing His name on our foreheads. *"And they shall see his face; and his name shall be in their foreheads"* (Rev. 22:4). What the Spirit of God is doing now in our lives is to conform us to the Lord's image. But once we possess glorified bodies this process of conformation will be perfected and we shall be like the Lord in all of His moral excellence.

Perfect Kingdom

The kingdom of God in eternity will be perfect without any rebellion or discord. *"And they shall reign for ever and ever"* (Rev. 22:5). Our reigning will not end with the consummation of the millennial kingdom, but will continue through eternity. We shall be assigned responsibilities in the eternal city.

PRESENT DAY IMPLICATIONS

1. Are you leaving your present life in the light of eternity?

2. What you see now will one day be burned up with fire and only what you did for the Lord will last.

3. Do not store up treasures on earth, but lay up your treasures in heaven.

4. If our future state is perfection, then what are we doing to pursue it?

DECISIONS

Write down the decisions that you made in light of this chapter.

_____

_____

_____

_____

_____

_____

SIX

HOW DO YOU FIT INTO GOD'S PLAN?

Now that you have read about God's plan from the present to eternity, it would be meaningful to engage in a spiritual exercise of evaluating your life in light of God's plan for the future. Basically, where do I stand in God's plan?

There is no book that reveals the future as the Bible does. It is reliable and trustworthy from the standpoint of accuracy and authority. The world events are moving in the direction that would conform to God's plan. Nations are aligning themselves to biblical prophecy.

EVALUATE YOUR LIFE BASED ON THE FOLLOWING QUESTIONS:

1. Do I believe the Bible as God's message to mankind?
2. If I do, am I going to obey what it says?
3. Where do I think I am in God's plan?
4. Will I be part of the rapture when Christ comes to gather His people to heaven?
5. Will I go through the Tribulation Period when God pours out His judgment?
6. Will I be part of the millennial kingdom of Christ?
7. Will I be part of the Great White Throne Judgment?
8. Will I be in Heaven forever?
9. Will I be in Hellfire forever?

WHAT CAN YOU DO NOW TO CHANGE YOUR LIFE AND ETERNAL DESTINY?

Repent of your ways

It means you are willing to change your life from your present condition to where God wants you to be. Your life in your sinful state is not acceptable to God. You need Jesus Christ in your life to bring about the change that He desires of you. Jesus said, *"for I am not come to call the righteous, but sinners to repentance"* (Matt. 9:13). *"Repent ye therefore, and be converted, that your sins may be blotted out, when the times of refreshing shall come from the presence of the Lord"* (Acts 3:19).

Confess your sins to God

It means to admit to God that you have broken God's commandments and laws. It means to agree with God that you are a sinner (one who has missed the mark or standard of God for your life) and worthy of God's judgment. It means you have sinned against God in your thought life, words, and deeds. *"If we confess our sins, he is faithful and just to forgive us our sins, and to cleanse us from all unrighteousness"* (1 John 1:9).

Believe in God's Son Jesus Christ

It means putting your trust in Jesus Christ to save you out of your present condition and to give you eternal life. He is the only one who can give you hope of eternal life and the prospect of spending eternity in heaven with Him. It means you are willing to put your confidence in what He has done on your behalf over 2,000 years ago, on the cross, to give you liberty from the bondage of sin and Satan. It means you are willing to accept His sacrificial death as the penalty for your sins. *"But these are written, that ye might believe that Jesus is the Christ, the Son of God; and that believing ye might have life through his name"* (John 20:31).

Accept Jesus Christ into your life

It means to invite Jesus Christ by faith into your heart as Saviour and Lord. It means to enthrone Him in your life as all in all. It means to allow the Lord Jesus to live in and through your life from this moment onwards. It means to enter into a personal relationship with Him that demands commitment to live and serve Him wholeheartedly. *"If thou shalt confess with thy mouth the Lord Jesus, and shalt believe in thine heart that God hath raised him from the dead, thou shalt be saved. For with the heart man believeth unto righteousness; and with the mouth confession is made unto salvation"* (Rom 10:9-10).

WHAT WILL GOD DO WHEN YOU TAKE THIS STEP OF ACCEPTING CHRIST INTO YOUR LIFE?

There are a lot of things that God will do on our behalf, of which a select few are listed below. Obviously, space limits me from listing all of the things that God initiates in the life of a sinner who comes to Him in repentance. And there are a lot more things that we will never know or comprehend.

Forgives all your sins

When you accept Jesus Christ into your life, God will honour your decision and do what His word promises, and that is, forgive all of your sins—past, present, and future. *"If we confess our sins, he is faithful and just to forgive us our sins, and to cleanse us from all unrighteousness"* (1 John 1:9).

Gives the Holy Spirit to live in you

The moment you submit to Christ, the Holy Spirit takes permanent residence in your heart. *"...he which stablisheth us with you in Christ, and hath anointed us, is God; Who hath also sealed us, and given the earnest of the Spirit in our hearts"* (2 Cor. 1:21-22).

Grants eternal life to you

God will grant you eternal life, which means you will live forever with God. *"And this is the record, that God hath given to us eternal life, and this life is in his Son. He that hath the Son hath life; and he that hath not the Son of God hath not life"* (1 John 5:11-12).

Grants entrance into the kingdom of heaven

God will grant you access into heaven and His kingdom. *"Verily, verily, I say unto thee, Except a man be born again, he cannot see the kingdom of God"* (John 3:3).

Removes the judgment of God from you

God will remove the condemnation and judgment, which would have led you into the eternal lake of fire. *"He that believeth on him is not condemned: but he that believeth not is condemned already, because he hath not believed in the name of the only begotten Son of God"* (John 3:18).

Declares you as righteous

God will declare that you are just and credits you with the righteousness of God, which is through Christ. *"Therefore being justified by faith, we have peace with God through our Lord Jesus Christ: By whom also we have access by faith into this grace wherein we stand, and rejoice in hope of the glory of God"* (Rom. 5:1-2).

Allows you to be born into the family of God

The Word of God and the Holy Spirit cause you to be born-again into the family of God. You become forever a child of God, never to be rejected or abandoned. *"But as many as received him, to them gave he power to become the sons of God, even to them that believe on his name"* (John 1:12).

Unites you as a member of the body of Christ

The Holy Spirit unites you into the body of Christ, which is Christ's church. *"For by one Spirit are we all baptized into one body, whether we be Jews or Gentiles, whether we be bond or free; and have been all made to drink into one Spirit"* (1 Cor. 12:13).

Blesses you with all spiritual blessings

The Heavenly Father blesses you with all spiritual blessings in Christ. *"Blessed be the God and Father of our Lord Jesus Christ, who hath blessed us with all spiritual blessings in heavenly places in Christ: According as he hath chosen us in him before the foundation of the world, that we should be holy and without blame before him in love: Having predestinated us unto the adoption of children by Jesus Christ to himself, according to the good pleasure of his will, To the praise of the glory of his grace, wherein he hath made us accepted in the beloved"* (Eph. 1:3-6).

Works in you to make you more like Christ

Christ will begin to work in you to conform you into His image, so that when you get to heaven you will be spotless and perfect. *"Being confident of this very thing, that he which hath begun a good work in you will perform it until the day of Jesus Christ"* (Phil. 1:6). *"And you, that were sometime alienated and enemies in your mind by wicked works, yet now hath he reconciled in the body of his flesh through death, to present you holy and unblameable and unreproveable in his sight"* (Col. 1:21-22).

If you make that decision to believe in Jesus Christ, then the awful judgment during the Tribulation Period will not come upon you nor will you stand at the Great White Throne Judgment to be judged into eternal hellfire. Instead your future will be secured by God, you will be raptured into heaven when Christ comes and you will be reigning with Christ in the millennial kingdom. You will spend your life forever in the eternal city enjoying the goodness of God.

APPENDIX

THE 70-WEEKS OF DANIEL

The 70-weeks of Daniel is a prophetic vision that God gave Daniel after he sought God's plan while in captivity in Babylon regarding the future dealings of God with His people—Israel. It outlines the general plan of God as far as timing is concerned and the major events that are going to take place in regard to Israel.

And whiles I was speaking, and praying, and confessing my sin and the sin of my people Israel, and presenting my supplication before the Lord my God for the holy mountain of my God; Yea, whiles I was speaking in prayer, even the man Gabriel, whom I had seen in the vision at the beginning, being caused to fly swiftly, touched me about the time of the evening oblation. And he informed me, and talked with me, and said, O Daniel, I am now come forth to give thee skill and understanding. At the beginning of thy supplications the commandment came forth, and I am come to shew thee; for thou art greatly beloved: therefore understand the matter, and consider the vision. Seventy weeks are determined upon thy people and upon thy holy city, to finish the transgression, and to make an end of sins, and to make reconciliation for iniquity, and to bring in everlasting righteousness, and to seal up the vision and prophecy, and to anoint the most Holy. Know therefore and understand, that from the going forth of the commandment to restore and to build Jerusalem unto the Messiah the Prince shall be seven weeks, and threescore and two weeks: the street shall be built again, and the wall, even in troublous times. And after threescore and two weeks shall Messiah be cut off, but not for himself: and the people of the prince that shall come shall destroy the city and the sanctuary; and the end thereof shall be with a flood, and unto the end of the war desolations are determined. And he shall confirm the covenant with many for one week: and in the midst of the week he shall cause the sacrifice and the oblation to cease, and for the overspreading of abominations he shall make it desolate, even until the consummation, and that determined shall be poured upon the desolate.   Daniel 9:20-27

WHAT IS THE 70-WEEKS OF DANIEL?

The Hebrew term "weeks" is used in Scriptures to denote a week of seven days or a week of seven years. *"And Laban said, It must not be so done in our country, to give the younger before the firstborn. Fulfil her week, and we will give thee this also for the service which thou shalt serve with me yet seven other years"* (Gen. 29:26-27).

From the time of the edict to rebuild the temple until they are restored to their land in peace under the kingdom rule of their Messiah, there is going to be 70 weeks, with the present age (church age) excluded from it because church was a mystery that was not revealed in the Old Testament.

A. The segments of the 70-week period

1. **Seven weeks**—Seven weeks is equivalent to 49 years (7x7). *"Know therefore and understand, that from the going forth of the commandment to restore and to build Jerusalem unto the Messiah the Prince shall be seven weeks"* (Dan. 9:25). King Artaxerxes issued the commandment to build Jerusalem on the 14th of March, 445 B.C. (Neh. 2:1-8). For the next seven weeks or forty-nine years,

the returned remnant built the city-walls and sanctuary in troublous times.

Major events during the 7-weeks:
- Command to build and restore Jerusalem

2. **Sixty-two weeks**—Sixty two weeks is equivalent to 434 years (62x7). Sixty-nine weeks from the edict to restore and build Jerusalem until Messiah the Prince was presented as Israel's king (Triumphal Entry into Jerusalem on March 30, A.D. 33 according to historians) and cutoff or killed in 483 years (49+434). *"And they brought him to Jesus: and they cast their garments upon the colt, and they set Jesus thereon. And as he went, they spread their clothes in the way. And when he was come nigh, even now at the descent of the mount of Olives, the whole multitude of the disciples began to rejoice and praise God with a loud voice for all the mighty works that they had seen; Saying, Blessed be the King that cometh in the name of the Lord: peace in heaven, and glory in the highest...And when he was come near, he beheld the city, and wept over it, Saying, If thou hadst known, even thou, at least in this thy day, the things which belong unto thy peace! but now they are hid from thine eyes"* (Luke 19:35-38, 41-42).

"Rejoice greatly, O daughter of Zion; shout, O daughter of Jerusalem: behold, thy King cometh unto thee: he is just, and having salvation; lowly, and riding upon an ass, and upon a colt the foal of an ass" (Zech. 9:9).

Major events during the 62-weeks:
- Messiah the Prince will be presented as Israel's king
- Rejection and crucifixion of the Messiah
- Destruction of the city of Jerusalem and the temple by Emperor Titus in AD 70. *"And Jesus went out, and departed from the temple: and his disciples came to him for to shew him the buildings of the temple. And Jesus said unto them, See ye not all these things? verily I say unto you, There shall*

not be left here one stone upon another, that shall not be thrown down" (Matt. 24:1-2).

3. **One week** – One week is equivalent to 7 years (1x7). The Antichrist will sign an accord or agreement with Israel (unbelieving Jews) to establish their temple and the inauguration of sacrifices. *"And he shall confirm the covenant with many for one week: and in the midst of the week he shall cause the sacrifice and the oblation to cease, and for the overspreading of abominations he shall make it desolate, even until the consummation, and that determined shall be poured upon the desolate"* (Dan. 9:27).

Major events during the 1-week:
- Between the sixty-ninth week and the beginning of the 70th week is the present age of the church, which was a mystery in the Old Testament.
- The 70th week will only begin after the church is raptured out of this world and the Antichrist signs an agreement with Israel. Then the prophetic clock will begin to tick again in regard to God's dealings with Israel, which has been suspended during the church age.
- During the middle of the week (3.5 years) the Antichrist will break his agreement with Israel and set himself up as god in the temple to be worshipped by all. *"When ye therefore shall see the abomination of desolation, spoken of by Daniel the prophet, stand in the holy place, (whoso readeth, let him understand:) Then let them which be in Judaea flee into the mountains"* (Matt. 24:15-16).

B. Accomplishments of the 70-weeks for Israel
1. To finish the transgression (God's judgment upon Israel for their sins will be completed)
2. To make an end of sins (Israel will repent of their sins when the Lord returns)

3. To make reconciliation for iniquity (Israel will be completely forgiven when it recognizes Christ as its Messiah)

4. To bring in everlasting righteousness (The millennial kingdom will be established which was promised to Israel)

5. To seal up vision and prophecy (All prophecies regarding Israel will be fulfilled)

6. To anoint the Most Holy (Restoration of temple worship)

DECISIONS

Write down the decisions that you made in light of this chapter.

_____

_____

_____

_____

_____

_____